Handspinning

Handspinning

Eliza Leadbeater

Photographs by Robert M. Eyres
and Lawrence A. Sands

Drawings by Alexandra Leadbeater

Studio Vista

London

A Studio Vista book published by
Cassell & Collier Macmillan Publishers Ltd
35 Red Lion Square, London WC1R 4SG
and at Sydney, Auckland, Toronto, Johannesburg
an affiliate of Macmillan Publishing Co. Inc., New York

Designed by Sally Muir
Filmset and printed by BAS Printers Limited,
Wallop, Hampshire

ISBN 0 289 70598.3

To Edna and Wes
   for making my dream a reality!

Contents

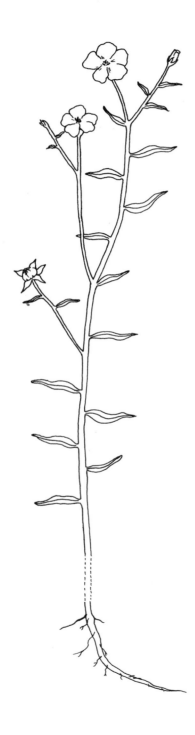

Acknowledgements 7

1 **Through the ages** 9

2 **Preparation for spinning** 19
  Preparation of fibres
  Arranging the fibres

3 **Spinning** 38
  Spindle
  Great wheel
  Treadle wheel

4 **Experimenting** 52
  With other techniques
  With other fibres

5 **Natural dyeing** 76
  Preparation for dyeing
  Mordanting
  Methods for dyeing wool

6 **Yarn design** 90
  Within fibre preparation
  Within spinning
  Preparing handspun for use
  Uses of handspun

Suppliers 104

Bibliography 107

Index 110

Acknowledgements

This book could not have materialized without the aid of numerous people on both sides of the Atlantic to whom I shall always be indebted for instilling in me a love for the art of spinning.

I wish to extend my thanks to Mr R. Patterson, Curator of the Castle Museum in York. Although unbeknown to him, years ago he kindled in me a great desire to know more about the art and craft of spinning. This dear gentleman set me on one of the greatest adventures I have yet to experience.

Warmest appreciation is felt towards my Canadian friends, Edna and Wes Blackburn of Caledon East, Ontario. Edna, a fountain of knowledge and patience, made my dream of spinning a thread a reality. The happy informative days spent at their farm treadling a variety of wheels, gathering dye materials from the hillside, stirring endless pots over the blazing fire in the dye-house, as well as mingling with their sheep and spinners from near and afar, will long be cherished. How thankful I am that a bit of pioneer life lingers in the beauty of the Canadian countryside!

To my husband, Christopher, thank you is not enough for his enthusiastic encouragement. His assistance was always present from the very beginning when he held my foot on the treadle so I could conquer the first barrier. I will appreciate always the hours he sacrificed from his own interests to repair and replace parts of wheels and textile tools, to sort fleeces, to identify and gather dye materials and to travel to historical places and museums both here and in America so that we could sketch and photograph bits and pieces of the past. I am indebted to him for his whole-hearted assistance in pursuit of my craft and in preparation of this book.

My thanks also must go to my families here and there, as well as my friends and the folk I have met in my travels who have endured listening to, questioning and testing my ideas.

Special appreciation extends to the many who have assisted me in the preparation of this book, especially

Robert and Alexandra for using their cameras and pens respectively with patience and talent, as well as to Mother who helped to get the manuscript into shape while Father prodded us all on. Thank you to my spinning friends, especially Rita Acton, Sylvia Hayes, Gordon Hocken and Tony Reid who always shared their ideas, as well as their work. My appreciation to my editors, Susannah Read for her guidance and Tim Cawkwell for his patience. Thank you all for your encouragement.

1 Through the ages

Spinning has remained relatively unchanged since man first discovered the process of twisting fibres into a continuous strand. No one can date the first appearance of the craft, but evidence of textiles has been found from the Early Stone Age when man discovered that his surroundings could provide him with fibrous materials such as wool, silk, cotton and flax which could be processed to clothe him. Just how spinning was invented will probably never be known, but it seems to have been discovered independently in different regions using alternative materials and must have resulted from observation and experimentation.

The primitive spindle is believed to have evolved from a stick used to store finger-spun yarn. It consisted of a slightly tapered stick (spindle) weighted with a whorl. The whorl could be at either end of this stick and

1.1 Byzantine spindle whorl with sheep and cross, AD 600 (Author's collection)

1.2 Top Row: Iron Age spindle whorls, stone, 1000–900 BC
Row 2 (left to right): Late Bronze Age, limestone/Byzantine, bronze/Late Bronze Age, pottery/Chalcolithic Period, stone
Row 3: Roman, glass, AD 300/Roman, ivory, 100 BC/Roman, amber, AD 300/Byzantine, alabasta, AD 600
Row 4: Roman, ivory whorls/Pre-Columbian, pottery/Pre-Columbian, stone
(Author's collection)

1.1

1.2

1.3   Direct drive spindle

Opposite
1.4   Accelerated spindle

took a variety of forms but was predominantly a disc or ball, shaped from stone, clay, bone, wood or glass. As the whorl functioned as a fly wheel, the weight and proportions of the spindle and whorl were determined by the type of fibres and yarn to be spun. Spinning of flax, for example, would require a heavier whorl than wool.

India is credited with one of the most important accomplishments, mechanizing the spindle. Although there is no confirmed date, some historians believe that around 500 BC an Indian wheel known as the charkha evolved from the reel employed in China for the unwinding of silk from cocoons. The spindle was mounted horizontally between two supports and rotated by a wheel having a continuous driving belt round it and driving the spindle with the whorl functioning as a pulley. It was not until the Middle Ages that this invention reached Europe. The charkha, now mounted on legs and known as a great wheel, is believed to have been introduced into Britain from Holland. Because it was used for wool spinning, it was often referred to as a wool wheel, although in Scotland it was referred to as a muckle wheel, and in Ireland as the long wheel. The American equivalent, larger in size but as primitive,

10

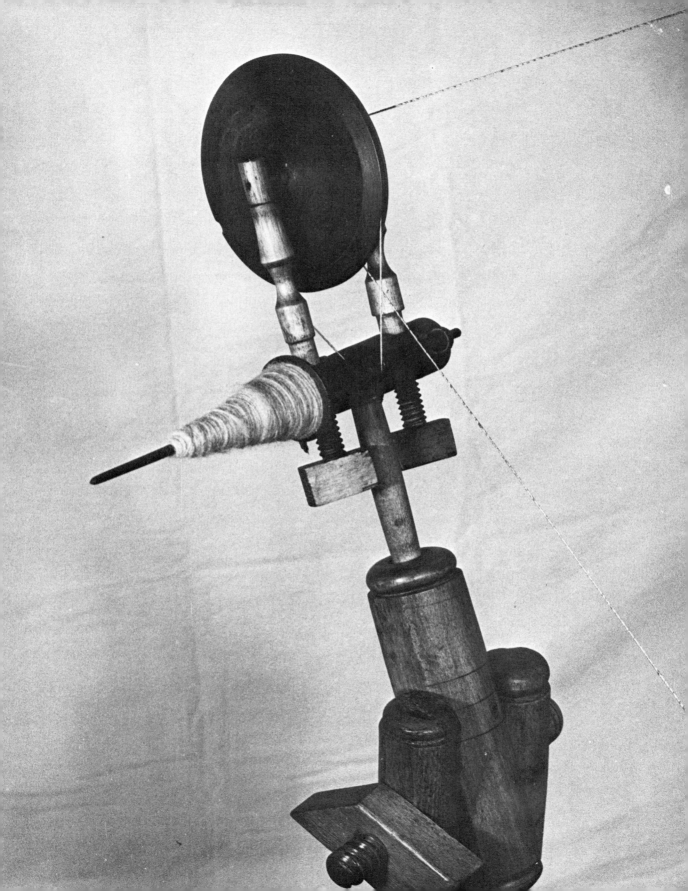

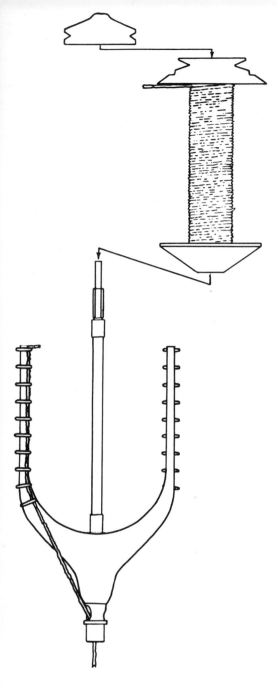

1.5 U-flyer and bobbin (Illustration M. Coolley)

Opposite
1.6 Early hand carders were dried teasels mounted on a rack with a handle; later they were used to raise the nap on woven fabric.

was the walking wheel. This wheel, usually made by the man of the family, consisted of a plank set on three legs with a perpendicular post at the front that held a large flat-rimmed wheel, usually made by the village cooper, which was used to drive the spindle directly. A later innovation that appeared in 1802 was an accelerated wheel head patented by Amos Minor of New York. The Minor's head, as the device became known, consisted of an intermediate pulley between wheel and spindle. The extra pulley was used to increase the speed of rotation of the spindle.

Although much faster than the spindle, these primitive wheels still provided an intermittent method of spinning, as winding remained a separate operation from spinning. Johann Jurgen, a German woodcarver, is credited with incorporating the spinning and winding in one operation in 1530 based on an earlier scheme devised by Leonardo da Vinci. The adaptation consisted of mounting a bobbin over the spindle and providing a U-shaped wooden arm or flyer to distribute the spun yarn on to the bobbin. Both flyer and bobbin were rotated by a single driving belt doubled round the wheel. The pulley on the bobbin was made smaller than that on the flyer so that the bobbin rotated faster than the spindle winding in the yarn as it was spun.

Numerous old wheels, diverse in style, can be found today. They can be classified as having either horizontally mounted spindles or bobbins and flyers. Their design generally reflects their place of origin, as well as being an indicator of age.

Fibre preparation prior to spinning is most important to the good quality of the finished yarn and archaeological finds show that early civilizations were skilled at fibre preparation. Different tools were developed for different fibres. The first step in wool preparation is shearing, a task that requires skill for the fibres must be removed from the sheep without injuring the animal. Bronze Age shepherds plucked the wool from the sheep, a technique still employed on the descendants of these animals today. Shears, in the form of two metal knives joined by a spring, first appeared during the Iron Age and have remained virtually unchanged. The activity was speeded up when mechanical shears operating on electricity and petrol were introduced. The wool fibres were next disentangled; the method used in prehistoric Europe was to beat the wool with a length of gut strung on a bow, but by classical times the processes of combing and carding were known.

The early carders are believed to have been dried teasels (*Dipsacus fullonum*) mounted on a cross. The term carding derives from the Latin *carduus* or teasel. Until recently the same sort of device has been used to

raise the nap on cloth. Wire teeth eventually replaced the teasels, but not until the thirteenth century do we have evidence of this. The making of handcards was a laborious task as hundreds of wire teeth had to be individually cut, bent and set into a leather backing which had been previously pierced to receive them. In 1797 an American, Amos Whittemore, invented a machine that turned out fully made card clothing suitable for handcarders and the new power carding machines. The principles of modern power carding were developed around 1738 by two Englishmen, Paul and Bourn, and led to the development of power driven carding machines, although it was not until the end of the eighteenth century that these machines appeared in America. England, on her rise as an industrial power, was eager to safeguard her inventions and prevent their use elsewhere so that the carding machines in use in America were reproductions of an inferior construction. They were driven first by water and later by steam. This invention, like the others that followed, removed the task of fibre preparation from the home to the increasing number of carding mills and was undoubtedly fundamental to the further development of the textile industry in both America and Britain.

It is regrettable that the introduction of machinery destroyed the craft of combing almost completely. Combing was employed from classical times for the preparation of flax and silk and later, wool. The wool combs that evolved by the nineteenth century were T-shaped handles set with two to five rows of tapered metal teeth. They weighed an average of 4 kilograms and were used in pairs, one was heated in a special stove while the other was attached to an iron pad, called a jenny, mounted on a vertical post. Combing required strength as well as skill, and was carried out by the craftsmen working in their own homes until their replacement by machinery in the nineteenth century.

The tools used for the preparation of flax have two purposes: to break up and remove the useless woody inner part of the stem and to comb and arrange the fibres preparatory to spinning. At first the breaking of the flax was achieved by beating the previously rotted and dried fibres with a wooden mallet which was succeeded around the fourteenth century by the flax break. The flax break consisted of a number of wooden knives mounted in a frame which were banged together to break up the flax stems. After breaking the flax was scutched or swingled by beating it with a wooden scutching knife to remove bits of boon left after breaking. The final operation was the combing of the fibres. The combs, called hackles or heckles, consisted of rows of pointed teeth set in a board. Hackling required the use of a sequence of combs having progressively finer teeth set at close intervals, the coarsest being used first.

The distaff was another aid for the spinner. Often it was nothing more than a stick held under the arm or secured in the belt on which prepared fibres were held for spinning. A similar device was added to the spinning wheel.

1.7 Because of the error in measurement that could be accumulated by using a niddy-noddy, the click reel was introduced. It had a definite circumference and a signalling mechanism to indicate the number of rounds.

After the yarn was spun it was necessary to remove it from the bobbin, measure it and store it in skeins until needed: the implement designed for this task was the reel. In its primitive form it consisted of a stick with two short arms at each end, but later a variation of this device was achieved when one arm was turned at a right angle to the other thereby making a skein twice the length. This was called a niddy-noddy and produced a skein usually two yards round. The error in measurement that could be accumulated by the niddy-noddy was quite considerable. In fact, its use was forbidden in Scotland in 1695 because of this wide margin of error. The click reel when introduced quickly replaced the stick reel as it had four or six arms of a definite circumference, generally two yards, and, although hand-operated, had a simple gear-like mechanism that would click, signalling forty rounds. After every forty rounds a knot would be tied; the number of knots making a skein varied with locality.

As a craft, spinning evolved into an honourable occupation, a duty which fell to women in early civilizations as the Old Testament records: 'She seeketh wool, and flax, and worketh willingly with her hands . . . She layeth her hands to the spindle, and her hands hold the distaff . . . She maketh fine linen.' (Proverbs 31:13, 19, 24.)

Little was recorded of the development of the textile industry in Britain prior to the sixteenth century, although manuscripts and merchants' accounts provide evidence that the making and selling of fine cloth was a thriving medieval industry. The wool industry that flourished, unaided by machinery, was entirely carried out by craftsmen in their cottages. The organizing force for all this industrial activity was a person known as a clothier. He had in his employment either his own family or the services of a large number of journeymen, apprentices and women. These employees worked at home and had their materials and perhaps equipment provided by the clothier. They usually worked for a piece-rate wage. Since at least five spinsters were required to keep one weaver fully supplied with yarn one can visualize the size of the clothier's unit. To produce a length of woven cloth, the clothier had first to buy his wool usually from a local farmer or, with larger consignments, from a wool dealer. After scouring, the wool would be prepared by carding or combing and given out to the spinsters for the making of yarn. A spinster working twelve hours per day could spin about a pound of medium yarn and her week's labour was brought to the 'takkin' in shop' where it would be given out to the weavers. After weaving, the cloth was finished by other craftsmen, fullers and dyers, employed by the clothier, or sold 'in the raw' (unfinished) to merchants throughout the country and from abroad.

With all its advantages the spinning wheel still had its limitations for it could only produce a single thread. In the latter part of the eighteenth century the need for a machine that could spin several threads at once was answered; it was invented by James Hargreaves, an English weaver. The introduction in 1765 of the spinning jenny, as Hargreaves' invention became known as, was the first step toward maintaining a quantity thread supply for the weaver and although it was to hasten the development of a textile industry in Lancashire, it brought bitter feelings from those who earned their living by the old mode of spinning. Several years later in 1769 Richard Arkwright patented his water frame. Although an improvement on Hargreaves' machine Arkwright is credited less with its invention, but rather with borrowing from the modifications of other spinners. The successful feature of Arkwright's machine was the use of drawing rollers which resulted in a more evenly drawn yarn that could be finer, yet strong enough to serve as a warp yarn. The cotton mule developed in 1779 by Samuel Crompton incorporated the movable carriage and spindles of the jenny with the roller drafting of the water frame resulting in a machine that could spin fine cotton yarn. Crompton's cotton mule was the prototype for the American spinning jack which by eliminating the roller drafting was suitable for wool spinning. It was not until inventions to hasten the production of yarn and cloth were introduced that the textile industry moved from the cottages to the factories, but not without much bitter misunderstanding on the part of those who had earned their living by using hand tools.

Although the Spanish explorers found beautifully produced cloth spun and woven by native people, the Pilgrims are credited with bringing spinning and weaving to the New World. Many of the early settlers had made cloth at home in Britain and were well acquainted with the process so it was not at all surprising that spinning wheels travelled to the new country.

Life for the early generations of settlers was rugged and even the necessities of life were scarce. Wool was also scarce and to meet the increasing demand for cloth, the growing of flax was encouraged and in some instances enforced by colonial legislation. For a long time it was ruled that every home have one spinner, and thus the entire family was involved with the raising of sheep and processing of flax, as well as carding, spinning and weaving. Even after the population of the colonies swelled, spinning and weaving continued to be carried on in the household, as families worked to supply cloth for their own use by their own manufacture. Unlike England, as a British Royal Governor of New York recorded in 1767, 'The custom of making these coarse cloths in private families prevails throughout the whole province, and almost in every house a sufficient quantity is manufactured for use of the family, without the least design of sending any of it to market.' (*Wool Technology and the Industrial Revolution*, Merrimack Valley Textile Museum, 1965.) The amount of homespun produced must have been quite considerable for in 1829 the textile manufacturers complained to the United States Congress about the amount done at home. Gradually the transition from home to factory took place between 1800 and 1840, although as late as 1850 many areas of the new country still had a large number of handspinners.

The woollen and cotton industries that flourished in both countries during the nineteenth century were aided by other inventions such as Whitney's cotton gin, mechanical pickers, carders and power looms. The industry flourished along with the economic activity and a profound change in productivity was achieved in a short time: where in 1770 one spinner with one spinning wheel could produce four skeins per day, by 1815 one spinner with one spinning jack produced seven hundred skeins. In fifty-five years a domestic industry so widely practised was suddenly changed; it moved from the fireside to the factory and progressed from hand to steam power.

Today restoration villages and folk museums continue to foster and aid the revival of this ancient craft. Even the non-spinner will find examples of old textile equipment a fascinating subject as they provide insight into the inventiveness of our ancestors and give a greater understanding of the craft and its transition from home to factory, as well as a greater appreciation of the people who developed it.

2 Preparation for spinning

A knowledge of the characteristics and spinning qualities of any fibre is essential before exploring its design potential. Wool, the most varied of a wide range of both natural and man-made fibres that handspinners today have the opportunity of using, provides exciting possibilities for yarn design.

Characteristics of wool

Wool originated with the domestication of sheep in the highlands of Mesopotamia. In examining the coat or fleece of a sheep the most evident characteristic of its wool is that it grows in cohesive groups of fibres which are called locks. A lock of wool is composed of thousands of individual fibres formed by the accumulation of dirt and natural grease and resembles a tuft which is bunched together at the top. The behaviour and properties of wool derive from the microscopic construction of these fibres. The surface of the wool fibre is composed of scales which overlap from the root in the direction of the tip (fig. 2.1) rather like the tiles of a roof overlapping from top to bottom. The formation of the scales is not uniform; in coarser wools there are fewer scales and less overlapping than in finer wools, which results in the points of the scales being further apart giving a more lustrous, hair-like appearance particularly evident in a breed such as Lincoln Longwool. This surface greatly

2.1 Microscopic structure of wool fibre showing overlapping scales

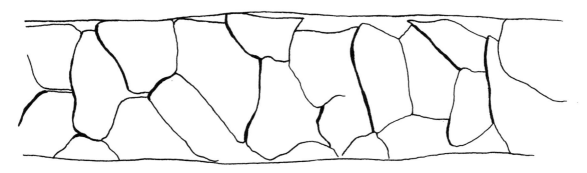

19

2.2 On examining the locks closely, it can be seen that the whole length is to some degree crimped. The degree of natural waviness varies between breeds: the Scottish Blackface has little (left) compared to the simple waviness of the Lincoln Longwool (right) and the complex crimp of the Southdown (centre).

facilitates the spinning of wool as the scales mesh together between individual fibres and produce a continuous interlocked yarn.

On casual observation, it can be seen that the whole length of a fibre to some degree possesses a natural waviness termed crimp. This crimped characteristic varies between breeds. Some wool fibres, such as Scottish Blackface, have little crimp, whereas the Lincoln Longwool has a simple waviness compared to the complex crimp of the Southdown (fig. 2.2). The amount of crimp in the fibre is another determining factor in the design potential of wool. Fibres with a great amount of crimp produce softer, more bulky yarns than those spun from fibres with little crimp from which a hard wiry yarn is produced. This natural waviness can never be completely overcome no matter how tightly the fibres are spun and it contributes to the resilience and warmth of the wool because of the entrapped air which allows the fibre to retain its elasticity, as well as warmth.

Sheep breeds are usually classified as mountain/hill, longwool/lustre and shortwool/down (fig. 2.2) which emphasize the nature of their surroundings and the character of the coverings they grow to protect themselves in these environments. Wool classifications differ between countries, although there is a world classification which places over forty breeds and more than two hundred recognized crossbreeds into five categories. Class One Wool includes merino stock with a staple from 2 to 12 cm. Class Two Wools possess a staple from 5 to 20 cm in length and includes numerous British breeds that are raised around the world. Wools with a staple from 10 to 30 cm are grouped in category three; these are British lustre wools. Class Four Wools include the half-breeds with irregular length staples, while Class Five is a non-sheep grouping for animals that are akin to sheep such as the Persian lamb. In the UK, a number system is employed by marketing boards and breeders to indicate the quality or fineness of the wool. The fineness is determined by the individual diameter of the wool fibres. The system is based on the assignment of 100 to the finest wool with lower numbers relating in proportion to coarser fibres. Although the system was introduced to assist the worsted yarn manufacturer, it does serve as a general guide for the handspinner as to the fineness of the wool. In the US a system of blood grades is employed to indicate the fineness of the fibre. This system incorporates seven standard blood grades: full blood, half blood, three eighths, one quarter, common, braid and britch. For the handspinner, it is best to judge the fibre on its own merit, not mainly on its degree of fineness, for every breed offers characteristics that can be employed differently in yarn design.

Preparation of fibres

Selection of a fleece

Having chosen a breed because of its characteristic qualities which the handspinner intends to exploit, the next stage is the selection of a fleece. Regardless of the breed chosen, there are factors which the handspinner must consider during selection. In the UK a spinner, unless he raises his own sheep, usually buys a fleece through the Wool Marketing Board. In many respects this can be advantageous, for this central clearing house attempts to maintain high standards, and wool purchased from this source is graded and therefore generally uniform in character. The beginner will find the staff most helpful as he can state the purpose for which the wool is required, for example a coarse rug or bulky knitting yarn, and they will assist in the selection if so desired. In North America the handspinner usually deals with either small independent marketing boards or with the farmer direct; this gives the benefit of being able to personally select a fleece that will offer no obstacles to spinning or quality of the yarn.

When choosing a fleece try to avoid the following:

Tender wool caused by sickness or even malnutrition of the animal. This can be checked by removing a lock and very lightly 'pulling' both ends simultaneously and observing if the lock breaks.

Second cuts, the short snips of wool coming from the coat the animal is growing for its next year's protection or more often the result of the shearer making a second pass as he removes the fleece, can be observed on the shorn surface of the rolled fleece. If present in excess they can add considerable problems to carding and spinning.

Excessive amounts of vegetation such as burr, twigs, etc. or dyemarkings which can be difficult to remove.

Over-dry weathered tips which are often weak and break during preparation.

Brittle or steely wool, as well as excessive kemp (a coarse protective hair which breeds in wet-districts produce to help shed the rain) which in excess can be the result of poor breeding.

Fleeces that are matted, felted or extremely dry.

Fleeces that are shorn and stored wet or damp.

Sorting a fleece

After selecting a fleece the next step is to sort it; this process is still done by hand even in the woollen industry. It is important to realize that wool sorting requires time. Before beginning it is necessary to clear a large area of floor space because once unrolled the fleece expands to a

Guide to sheep breeds

	Classification	Quality number	Staple length (centimetres)	Fleece weight (kilograms)	Suitability
Border Leicester	L	40–46	15–25	3–4.5	Knitting wool, dress fabrics
Cheviot	M	50–56	10	2	Liable to kemp. Woollens, tweeds
Clun Forest	D	56–58	7–10	2.5	Woollens, knitting wool
Columbia	C	50–56	10–13	4.5–5	Woollens
Corriedale	C	50–56	10+	4.5–5.5	Woollens, weaving, knitting
Cotswold	L	44–46	20–30	4	Worsted, coarse but lustrous
Dalesbred	M	32–40	20	2	Carpet, tweed yarns
Dartmoor	L	36–40	25–30	6–7.5	Tweeds, woollens
Derbyshire Gritstone	M	50–56	15–20	2–2.5	Knitting wool
Devon Closewool	D	46–50	7–10	2.5–3	Liable to kemp. Tweeds
Devon Longwool	L	32–36	25–30	6–7	Carpet, tweed, worsted
Dorset Down	D	56–58	8	2–2.5	Knitting wool
Dorset Horn	D	54–58	8–10	2–2.5	Fine tweeds, knitting wools
Exmouth	M	50–56	8–10	2–3	Tweeds, good felting
Hampshire Down	D	56–58	5–8	2–2.5	Knitting
Herdwick	M	28–32	13	1.5–2	Liable to kemp. Range of colours, carpet, tweed
Jacobs	M	48–54	13–20	2–3	Colour mottled white to black
Kent-Romney Marsh	L	48–56	15–18	4–4.5	Knitting wool, worsted, woollen
Kerry Hill	D	56–58	8–10	2–2.5	Knitting wool, fine tweed, furnishing
Leicester	L	40–46	13	5–6	Rugs, furnishing
Lincoln Longwool	L	38–44	30–40	5–6.5	Worsted
Llanwenog	D	56–58	13	1.5	Knitting, fine tweed

M = Mountain/D = Down/L = Longwool/C = Cross bred

	Classification	Quality number	Staple length (centimetres)	Fleece weight (kilograms)	Suitability
Lonk	M	32–44	10–15	2–2.5	Knitting wool, tweeds, blankets
Masham	C	40–42	18–35	2.5–3	Worsted
Merino	D	62+	6–8	variable	Woollen. Quality depends on variety
North County Cheviot	M	50–56	7–8	2	Tweeds
Orkney	D	50–56	2–8	variable	Woollen
Oxford Down	D	50–58	15	3.5–4.5	Knitting wool
Radnor	D	50–58	8–18	2	Liable to kemp. Woollen, tweeds
Rambouillet	D	62–70	6–8	4	Fine, soft. Woollen
Rough Fell	M	32–36	20	2	Carpet
Ryeland	D	56–58	8–10	2.5–3.5	Knitting, fine tweed
Scottish Blackface	M	28–32	20–33	2–3	Carpets, tweeds
Shetland	D	56–60	8–10	1	Range of colours, wool rooed. Fine, soft. Knitwear, tweeds
Shropshire	D	50–58	9–11	2.5–3.5	Woollen, knitting
South Devon	L	36–40	18	5.5–7	Carpet, upholstery
Southdown	D	56–60	5–8	2.5	Knitting, tweed
Suffolk	D	54–58	5–8	2–3	Knitting, tweed
Swaledale	M	28–32	15–24	1.5–3	Carpet yarn, bulkier knitting, tweed
Teeswater	L	40–48	30	5.5–7	Worsted, carpet, tweeds
Welsh Mountain	M	36–50	5–10	1.5	Liable to kemp. Fine quality – tweed; coarser – carpet.
Welsh Mt. Black	M	36–50	8–10	1.5	Woollens, knitting
Wensleydale	L	40–48	35	5.5–7	Worsted
Whiteface Dartmoor	L	30–40	25–30	5.5–7	Coarse. Carpet, tweeds

M = Mountain/D = Down/L = Longwool/C = Cross bred

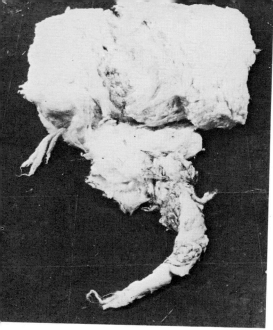

2.3 Partially unrolled fleece showing neck band

2.4 Fleece unrolled to its full length

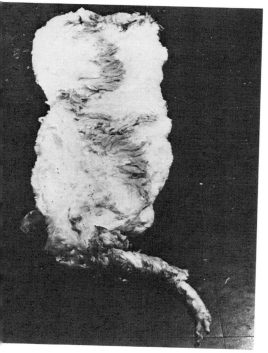

remarkable size. If the fleece is bought from a breeder who takes pride in his product, it comes carefully folded in a standard manner. The shorn ends will be outward as the fleece has been folded lengthwise in three and then tightly rolled starting from the tail or haunches and secured by a band of fleece made from pulling and twisting the neck and some shoulder wool into a braid. This neck band is then wrapped about the roll and its end secured by being tucked under itself.

First find the neck band and gently loosen it (fig. 2.3). Once the band is released unroll the fleece to its full length (fig. 2.4) and then open each side. When the sides are unfolded the sorter should be faced with the fleece properly laid out, that is, the tips of the wool locks facing upwards and the part of the fibres which were closest to the sheep before shearing touching the floor (fig. 2.5). Carefully untwist the neck band and then compact the fleece, if it has been over-stretched, to resemble the sorting diagram (fig. 2.6).

Now examine the wool to find a basis for sorting. A handspinner at this stage is exercising control over the yarn design by selecting the type of fibre which possesses the characteristics essential in the specific yarn to be spun. The reference for sorting may be fineness, crimp, length, lustre, strength or texture in handling. Since the natural elements such as weather affect the fleece and the quality of the fibre when it comes to dyeing and spinning, begin the actual sorting with this in mind, as well as the other characteristics, such as length of staple, which may be sought.

With reference to the diagram on the parts of a fleece (fig. 2.7), begin by sorting or skirting the poorest qualities first. This is frequently done by the breeder, but if not, it will include the legs, britch, belly area and head. These are usually too poor for spinning and often so terribly dirty that they are useless even for dyeing. Initially after removing the skirting by pulling the unwanted sections away with the hands, sort the fleece into three broad qualities.

The prime, which is the top rump and hind quarters, is better quality than the britch yet still poor because of exposure to weather and vegetation. If not too dirty, it is suitable for a coarse yarn or blending (see Chapter 6). The diamond area, which is the back and rear-back regions of the sheep, is second best and can be detected because of its lack of natural oils that have been removed by exposure to the weather. This lack of lanolin and weathered appearance is evident both visually and tactually and although a diagram of the fleece is helpful, these senses are the best guide to use in determining the extent of this grade.

24

2.5 Unrolled fleece with one side opened

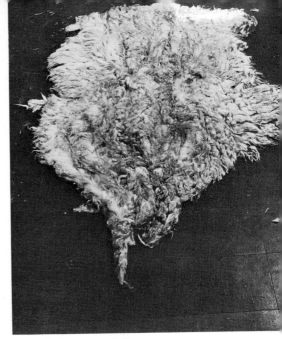

2.6 Fully opened fleece

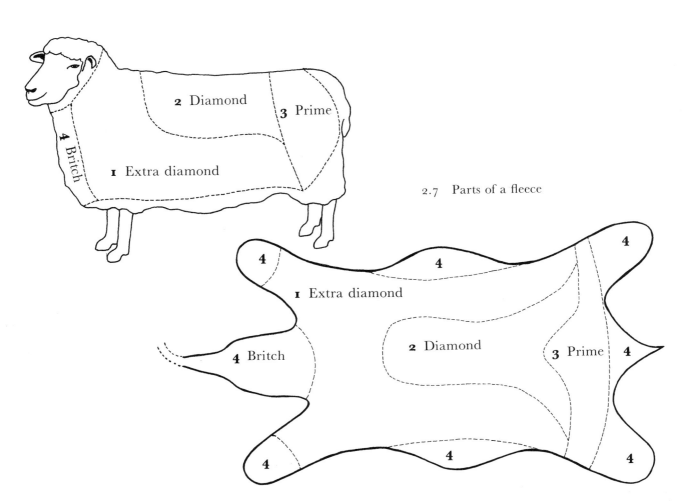

2.7 Parts of a fleece

2 Diamond

3 Prime

4 Britch

1 Extra diamond

4

4

4

1 Extra diamond

4 Britch

2 Diamond

3 Prime

4

4

4

4

What remains are the sides and shoulder sections including part of the neck band. This is the best quality wool and is referred to traditionally as extra diamond. This grade retains most of its natural oils and will look and feel softer, finer and greasier to the sorter's touch. After this preliminary sorting, the wool can be stored in these grades or further sorted by lock according to the handspinner's requirements.

As previously cautioned, the handspinner is wise to give considerable time to the process of sorting as an essential stage in preparation. By taking the time, some problems that can result from an inefficient or rushed job can be avoided. Care during sorting can remove the problems of excessive vegetation and dirt which are sometimes beyond scouring or carding, weak fibres that render a spun yarn useless, irregularity in felting which will affect the appearance of a finished article, unevenness in dyeing as different grades sometimes have varying affinities for dyes, or a variation in shrinkage rates caused when fibres having different degrees of crimp are not properly mixed.

It often happens that the handspinner is confronted with a fleece that has not been rolled in the standard manner, particularly if it has been opened for inspection. In this case arrange the wool as carefully as possible before starting and then rely on visual and tactile senses for sorting. It should also be noted that terms for grades vary between woollen and worsted sorters, as well as regions, so reference to the grade as best, seconds, thirds, poor or even hopeless is sufficient for the average spinner's use.

After sorting it is necessary to store the wool until it is needed. Whether scoured or in the grease, wool needs to breathe and for this reason the use of an old cotton pillow case is ideal, with tissue or newsprint separating the labelled grades if only one case is available. Wool is prone to attack by clothes moths particularly when it has been scoured. However, if the spinner is wise and purchases only what he can reasonably handle in a year, he will find no trouble in storing wool. Fleeces kept for longer periods often harden and mat, making the preparation difficult and time consuming. If the wool is to be kept over a year scour it, dry it properly and store as previously suggested in a pillow case with the addition of moth balls, and mark it according to breed and grades.

Scouring

There are as many theories on washing raw wool as there are spinners. Some spinners maintain that it must be washed at a certain temperature, others advocate particular scouring agents and then there are the purists who vow that the fibres must only be spun in the grease.

26

Wool is much easier to spin in the grease and for the beginner more rapid progress will be made by spinning the better grades of wool without scouring. There are occasions, however, when the wool should be scoured before spinning, for example when the wool is to be dyed prior to spinning or when it is excessively dirty or been stored for a long period.

Scouring is best approached in much the same manner as hand-washing woollens.

Tease or pick the wool to be scoured in an attempt to remove as much vegetation as possible and also to open the matted and weathered tips.

Enter the fibres into a laundry bowl or tub of hand-hot sudsy water containing a mild, well-dissolved soap, allowing it to soak for a short time to release the dirt.

Drain and prepare a second bath at the same temperature, but this time provide a gentle agitation by hand as well as removal by picking of anything that is lodged or tangled in the wool.

Unless the wool needs a third bath rinse it in clear hot water of the same temperature as the scouring bath and squeeze or gently press it to remove the excess water.

With long wools, scouring can take the form of steeping overnight in a bath which will open the locks. A second or third scouring at hand temperature can follow the next day. Either spread the wool to dry on a net frame or drape it over lines and bushes so that the air can circulate underneath. It can be placed in a mesh bag which is tightly secured and gently tumble-dried by machine at low temperature to prevent yellowing or other damage to the fibres by temperature extremes. The former is the safer method, but the latter is time-saving.

Experience shows that when scouring wool, or any fibres, there are several things to avoid. Harsh scouring agents can strip the fibre of all its natural oils and if not properly dissolved can cling to the fibres even after drying. Extreme temperature differences from one bath to another, as well as rough handling or agitation of wool, can cause felting. Finally, poor drying either by extreme or insufficient heat can be injurious to the fibres.

The next stage in the preparation of wool depends on the preference of the handspinner, for many choose to dye the wool prior to spinning. Dyeing with natural materials is discussed in Chapter 5.

Oiling

The scouring of an excessively dirty fleece removes the natural oils and some spinners find it advantageous to recondition the scoured fibres with oil. There are several ways of doing this. The easiest is to keep the finger tips lightly greased with an olive-oil emulsion. To prepare a quantity of fibre, sprinkle the olive-oil emulsion over the teased fleece from a spray bottle and blend through the fibres by reteasing. To prepare this emulsion, mix three parts olive oil with one part water and whip with a hand food mixer. After spraying, the teased wool is best stored in a cloth overnight and then reteased or carded. Oiling is not essential for with practice the skill can be acquired to draft and spin scoured fibres. Scour yarns that have been spun from artificially oiled fibres as soon as possible, as the oil can go rancid.

Arranging the fibres

The type of yarn spun is determined by the method used to arrange the fibres. Since the aim is to produce a controlled yarn, it is necessary to arrange the fibres in a consistent manner. This regularity can be obtained through the process of teasing the wool. The method of teasing takes a variety of forms, but carding or combing are the usual means employed to achieve a consistency in the fibre supply.

Carding

Carding is a method of both straightening and arranging the fibres. Handcarding involves the use of two wooden or metal paddles which have a special cloth consisting of bent wire teeth mounted on one side so that the paddles can be worked as a pair with the wool pulled and straightened between them.

The main criteria to use when selecting a pair of handcarders is the quality of card clothing. The wire teeth should be firm and lightly sharpened so that they are able to perform their task over a long period without damage to the fibres being carded. Fine wools need more delicate card clothing with a higher number of teeth per centimetre than coarse wools. If only one pair of handcarders is to be used a set with 4 to 5 teeth per centimetre (12 to 13 per inch) provides a good all-purpose carder suitable for use with a wide range of fibres. It is advisable to mark one carder left and the other right and use them accordingly in these hands for eventually they will wear differently.

Carding involves several preparatory stages prior to the actual use of the carders. First gather sufficient wool for the project required, selected on the criteria previously discussed. Even with the cleanest fibres, free from excessive foreign matter, there is usually a 25% weight loss in scouring. This percentage is further increased by fibres lost during the early teasing stages of

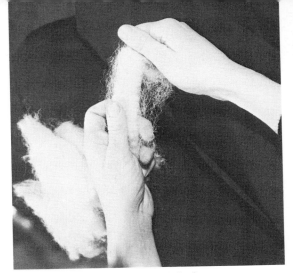

2.8 Testing the shorn ends before teasing

2.9 Removing second cuts

carding. The final weight loss can be as high as 45% for woollen spinning and much higher for worsted where the short fibres are removed. In planning a project calculate the amount needed from the beginning when fibre selection takes place starting with about twice that required for the project.

Assuming that the handspinner has the amount of materials required, first examine each lock by checking for second cuts, then rechecking for weak fibres. To do this hold the lock in one hand and tug at the shorn end (fig. 2.8). Any second cuts (fig. 2.9) will pull away and should be discarded unless being saved for use in a novelty thread. Having checked for and removed these bits, next open up the matted tips. Gently separate the fibres until they no longer resemble a lock but rather a light wispery strand (fig. 2.10). Since one of the purposes of this step is to remove additional foreign matter and release matted fibres, it is important that a method is developed for doing this, that is, wispery bits fall to the floor and the foreign bits to the spinner's apron or vice versa. Having prepared a good proportion of the fibres by teasing, a further blending can be employed to cause the fibres to become more uniformly mixed (fig. 2.11). Blending can be quite critical when it comes to mixing combinations of fibres, fibre lengths or crimp and this is dealt with more fully in Chapter 6. Having sufficiently teased and picked the fibres by hand it is now necessary to impose a regularity to the fibres while further fluffing them and this is achieved by use of the carders.

If the spinner remembers that the purpose of carding, in addition to removing foreign matter or vegetation, is to untangle, fluff, straighten and arrange the fibres so that they lie in a uniform direction then there should be little difficulty in recalling what to do at each stage.

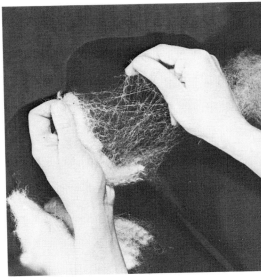

2.10 Teasing open the locks

2.11 Blending

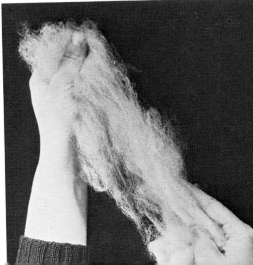

29

2.12 Stage 1: filling the left carder.

2.13 Stage 2: adding a second row of teased fibres.

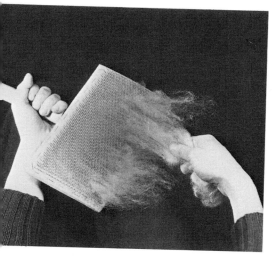

2.14 Stage 3: drawing fibres on to the right carder.

Stages of Carding

1 To begin, place the left carder on the lap and gather a handful of teased fibres in the right hand. Starting at the edge furthest from the handle fill the carder with small tufts of fibres (fig. 2.12).

2 Continue by making a second row slightly above the first. At this stage, the carders should not be covered beyond half their depth (fig. 2.13).

3 Take the empty right-hand carder and working from the end of the fibres on the left carder gently draw fibres on to the right carder (fig. 2.14). Continue this action by working 'up' the left carder – it is unnecessary to dig with the carders (fig. 2.15). Remember to take care when laying the right carder across the left, so that the fibre ends on the right carder are not curled under which will defeat the entire process as the result will be more tangled than the original wool (fig. 2.16).

4 When the fibres on the left carder can no longer be transferred to the right by brushing it is necessary to strip the fibres off the left carder on to the right. To do this place the left-hand carder a little above and parallel to the right-hand carder with its back towards the right-hand teeth. Engage the wool sticking out from the left-hand carder in the teeth of the right towards the upper part of the carder near to the handle. (This can be facilitated by pressing the fibres down lightly with the palm of the right hand.) Now draw the left-hand carder away at first keeping the carders approximately parallel but as this carder moves away turning it until the teeth are at right angles (fig. 2.17). Moving the left-hand carder down below the level of the right-hand one also aids in this stripping process.

5 All the fibres are now on the right-hand carder and the brushing operation across the left begins again starting at the edge of the carder and progressing to about three-quarters of the depth, never more (fig. 2.18).

6 When the fibres can no longer be transferred from the right carder it should then be stripped so all the fibres lie on the left carder (fig. 2.19).

7 Begin brushing again (fig. 2.20) as in Step 3 and when the fibres can no longer be transferred from the right-hand one Step 6 is repeated. Repeat these two steps, 3 and 6, of brushing and stripping, two or more times until the stage where the fibres are straightened and no 'tangled ridge' of fibres appears on the carder or across the edge.

The next step after the fibres are straightened is to remove them from the carders. There are several methods of accomplishing this, although most spinners have their own preference. One method is to strip the carded fibres that have accumulated on the left carder on to the right carder, so that this fluffy pad of wool rests lightly

30

2.15   Stage 3: continue drawing fibres on to the right carder by working 'up' the left carder.

2.16   The direction of laying the fibre ends during carding

2.17   Stage 4: transferring the fibres remaining on the left carder to the right one by stripping.

2.18   Stage 5: all the fibres have been transferred to the right carder. Carding on to the left begins.

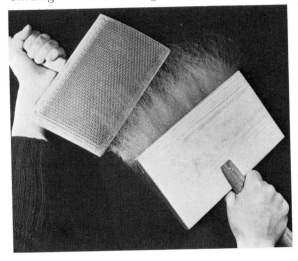

2.19   Stage 6: transferring the fibres remaining on the right carder to the left one by stripping.

2.20   Stage 7: continue drawing fibres on to the right carder as in Stage 3.

2.21   Forming the rolag on the back of the left carder

2.22   Using the teeth of the right carder to lift the fibres to start forming a rolag

2.23   Rolag being formed on the left carder by the lifting and stripping action of the teeth of the right carder

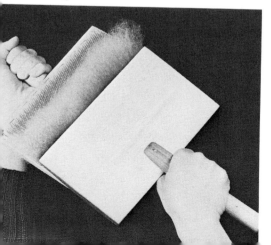

on the right carder. This pad is then deposited on the back of the left carder and then with the back of the right carder the fibres are rolled into a tube-like construction called a rolag (fig. 2.21). This is an easy technique but much more time consuming than the method of forming the rolag in one operation whilst stripping the wool. This stripping technique requires practice for it involves lifting the wool from the carder by the use of the teeth of the right carder (fig. 2.22). As the fibres are lifted in the stripping, they are also rolled with the carder and hand, if necessary, to form the rolag (fig. 2.23).

The fibres in the rolag lie perpendicular to its length trapping air inside the tube. This trapped air contributes to the spongey texture of the carded wool and when yarn is spun from wool prepared by this technique it is termed woollen.

Combing

Worsted spun yarn is the result of a different technique of fibre preparation called combing in which the fibres are so arranged that they lie parallel to each other and along the direction of the yarn when spun. Since this technique also removes the shorter fibres called noils, the spun yarn is characteristically smoother and firmer, less hairy and also cooler as the parallel arrangement traps less air to hold warmth.

Handcombing, once an important craft in the worsted regions of Yorkshire, is not a technique employed by many handspinners today since the equipment has not been readily available. However, handcombs are once again appearing on the market in modified versions of the old combs. Combing operates on the same principle as carding in that the fibres are straightened by transferring them from one comb to the other. Before combing begins, scour the fibres since if this is not done the lanolin in the wool sticks the fibres together and coats the comb's teeth making the operation very difficult.

Place one comb in an iron pad which is mounted horizontally. Pull the scoured wool lock by lock onto the comb, a technique called 'donning on' (fig. 2.24).
Now swing a second comb in a vertical motion and bring it closer to the mounted comb with each swing while drawing the wool from the static comb, a technique known as 'jigging' (fig. 2.25).
After the fibres have been transferred remove any short fibres (noilage) (fig. 2.26). These fibres are often still of suitable length to be woollen prepared and spun.
Exchange the positions of the combs and draw off the long fibres in the filled comb in a parallel arrangement.

32

To produce a more even finished product, draw off the long fibres from the combs at this point, divide them into lengths of 20 to 25 cm and repeat the donning on and combing process.

Continue combing until (a) all the fibres are straightened at which point the finished top will contain a mixture of long and shorter fibres or (b) all the short fibres are removed leaving an arrangement consisting only of long fibres.

Take off the combed fibres by drawing them through a 'diz', a piece of horn or leather containing a hole (fig. 2.27). This process both reduces the density of the fibres and acts as a check for short ends. The final arrangement is called a top.

2.24   Donning on the wool fibres

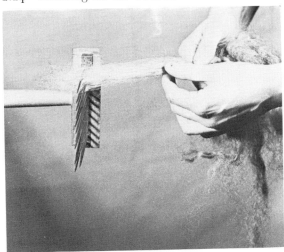

2.25   Jigging

2.26   The long fibres are transferred leaving the noils

2.27   Drawing off through the diz to form a top

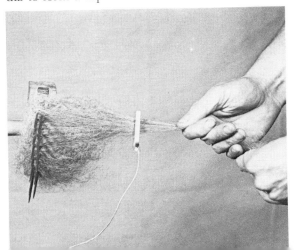

2.28 Flicking the end of a lock through the wool hackle

2.29 Noils remaining after withdrawing the lock from the hackle

Tops can also be prepared by taking a lock of wool which has had its tip opened and drawing it in a flicking manner through a wool hackle, dog's comb or carder several times from both ends (figs. 2.28, 29). This is a simplified method of preparing a worsted-type fibre supply, but it has several disadvantages apart from the small quantities which can be prepared. First, it does not satisfactorily remove the shorter fibres and, although this simple method serves to straighten and arrange the fibres in a parallel direction, it is more difficult to consistently piece and draft the fibres while spinning so that they maintain this worsted arrangement. For this reason, a real worsted yarn cannot be consistently managed from fibres prepared in this manner but a pleasant yarn called semi-worsted can be produced.

2.30 Opening the matted tip and end of the lock

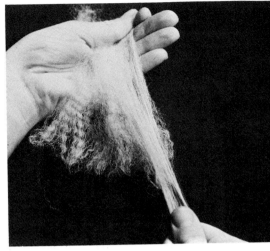

2.31 Shorn end secured between the thumb and index finger

Another technique which also produces a semi-worsted yarn is teasing. Teasing requires no equipment as it involves only the hands.

First take a lock as previously illustrated (fig. 2.8), check for second cuts and open the matted tips (fig. 2.30). Reverse the lock in the hand so that the shorn end is secured between the thumb and index finger (fig. 2.31). With the fingers of the other hand, draw the fibres away and with each pull gather a few fibre tips from the lock (fig. 2.32).

The end product should be a continuous roving with the fibres for the most part lying parallel to one another along the length.

This technique of preparation retains all the fibres regardless of length and in drafting and spinning there is no absolute consistency in the parallel arrangement. Having prepared the fibres by the technique which will best develop the characteristics desired in the yarn the fibres are ready to be spun!

2.32 Drawing the lock into a roving

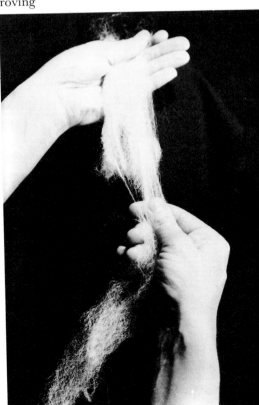

Glossary

Broken-mouthed: sheep unable to graze because the teeth are worn and therefore sold for meat.

Cast: badly bred or low quality wool.

Daggings, doddings, shirlings, crutchings, muck lumps, clarts: some of the many terms used for the dried lumps of dung and earth which cake the staples in the britch region.

Ewe: female sheep.

Fallen/fell wool: wool removed from skins of dead sheep, which is inferior in all aspects to fleece wool.

Fineness (Degree of): the diameter of the wool fibre which is designated by a quality number, 100 being assigned to the finest. Most British wools are classified between 28s to 60s. The fineness assists in determining the use of the wool and also the length of yarn that can be spun from a given weight.

Handle of wool: harshness or softness of the fibres.

Hogg, hoggets: wool from the first shearing of a long-wool or lustre breed yearling. It is the longest, finest and best quality fleece the sheep will produce.

Kemp: brittle and coarse white fibres of irregular length grown by poorly bred sheep or those raised in wet regions. Kemp absorbs dye poorly, and can be very evident in spun yarn.

Lustre (Degree of): amount of sheen or gloss on the fibres.

Rooed: plucked, rather than sheared, wool.

Springiness (Degree of): extent to which wool, after being compressed, will return to its natural bulk.

Staple length: length of the unstretched staple from base to tip.

Strength: ability of the fibres to resist breakage during processing. The wool is either sound or tender.

Suint: dried perspiration that encrusts the sheep's fibres.

Tegs: wool from the first shearing of down or mountain yearling.

Tup/ram: male sheep. Its wool is usually longer than the ewe.

Two-shear/toothed: denotes the number of clippings. The third shearing would make the ewe three toothed.

Wether/wedder: castrated male sheep. In England it also means wool other than first shearing.

Yield: amount of wool fibre remaining after scouring of natural grease and vegetation.

3 Spinning

Spinning, either by hand or power, involves the drawing or drafting of fibres to a required thickness while inserting a regular number of twists for strength. The yarn design is affected by the manner in which this is done. However, regardless of the yarn design or spinning technique, the spinning operation has three distinct divisions. These are:

a Fibre supply which can take various forms, woollen, worsted, etc., but whatever form is employed it should result in a uniformly arranged group of fibres from which a selection of fibres is later drawn to produce a yarn of a certain thickness or count. It is essential that the supply be easy to handle and that the fibres can be readily drawn out during drafting.

b Drawing out/drafting zone is the most critical stage for the number of fibres contained in this region determines the count of the yarn. If uniform results are required, then the number of fibres in this region must be kept as constant as possible.

c Twisting zone is the point at which friction (twist) is imposed on the drafted fibres thereby enabling them to cling together. This controlled cohesion forms the yarn. A guide to the amount of twist required is to make certain that sufficient friction is imposed to give the fibres cohesion and produce a yarn of required strength. The heavier the yarn the less the amount of twist required.

With an understanding of these basic principles, the handspinner has the concept of all spinning techniques regardless of the means used for imposing this twist.

3.1 The spinning operation has three distinct divisions: 1) the fibre supply 2) the drawing out or drafting zone 3) the twisting zone.

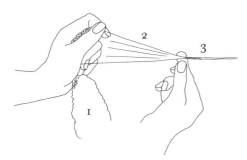

Spindle

Besides being widely available or easily made, the spindle has the advantage that it is easily portable and provides the spinner with the opportunity of seeing the basic principles unfold. Although a spindle appears to be nothing more than a weight with a hole (whorl) and a stick, there are finer points to consider in their selection or making. The design and size of the whorl should take into consideration the requirements of the spinner and the physical properties of the fibres to be spun. The spindle imparts the twist to the fibres from the rotational energy stored in its motion. The continued rotation of the spindle depends on its weight and shape. If the whorl is heavy and has its mass distributed on its periphery, it will continue to rotate for a long time and so the spinner can work uninterrupted. Such a design would seem ideal. However, if the whorl is large, the fibres have insufficient strength to support the spindle as they are being drafted and either a thick uneven yarn is produced or frequent breakages occur. It must also be remembered that as spinning progresses the weight of the yarn on the spindle increases, raising the overall spindle weight. For these reasons, a spindle with a large, heavy whorl is suitable for a beginner as it will spin well when empty and is easy to control. These spindles are also ideal for spinning tough coarse fibres, particularly hair fibres which tend to resist twisting. Their defect lies in their large weight which when increased by the spun yarn soon reaches the maximum the fibres can tolerate.

The ideal spindle is one where there is a good balance between the whorl and stick. The overall weight which includes the spun yarn should be no greater than what the fibres can support. The shape of the whorl is not as critical as with a heavy whorl, but it is advantageous that the weight be near the base of the tool. This can be achieved not only by using a dense material for the whorl, but also by providing additional weight by the use of a tapered stick. No one spindle will be suitable for the spinning of all fibres. The final requirement, although not essential, is that the stick has some form of a notch at the top. This is an aid in preventing the half-hitch on the spun yarn from slipping. A knob-like end is suitable for either S or Z twist spinning.

To use

A starting length will be required and it is best if this can be a piece of handspun yarn as it is often difficult to join on to commercially prepared yarns especially if they are plied. If a suitable length is not available, a piece can be made by finger spinning a small quantity of the prepared fibres. To do this draw out a small

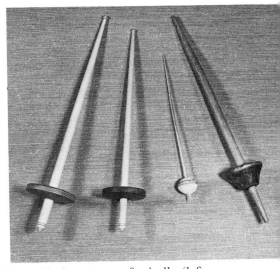

3.2 Various types of spindle (left to right):
Heavy: strong fibres / average: general purpose / small: pottery, for light fibres / peasant: an old Greek wool spindle.

quantity of fibres and twist in a clockwise direction with the fingers (fig. 3.3); this will produce a short length of yarn which can be tied to the top of the spindle and spinning can commence.

Rotate the spindle in a clockwise direction by flicking its end between the thumb and index finger whilst holding the fibre supply in the other hand, usually the left (fig. 3.4).

The object is to control the number of fibres being twisted and the amount of twist put into them. Do this by working both hands in unison: draw out and draft the fibres with the left hand controlling the fibre supply, and control the quantity of twist allowed to enter the fibre supply with the right-hand thumb and index finger by squeezing them together lightly over the spun yarn above the twist and below the drafting zone.

Draw the left hand upwards and attenuate the fibre supply immediately above the right hand. Gently release the pressure of the right-hand fingers to allow the twist through to the attenuated region, twisting up these fibres and producing a spun yarn as the right hand slides up the twisting fibres towards the fibre supply. During the whole operation of drafting and sliding, keep the spindle rotating in a clockwise direction (Z twist) by using the fingers of the right hand.

Spin a length about 40 to 50 cm (20 in) long, and slip the tied start of the spun yarn down towards the spindle whorl.

Holding the tapered end of the spindle in the right hand and the spun yarn tensioned in the left, wind on several centimetres (2 in) of yarn in a clockwise direction (fig. 3.5).

Take the yarn across and under the whorl and around the base of the stick (fig. 3.6). Following the illustrations (figs. 3.7, 8) make a half-hitch to secure the yarn to the spindle, leaving several centimetres of yarn available beyond the tip so spinning can continue as before.

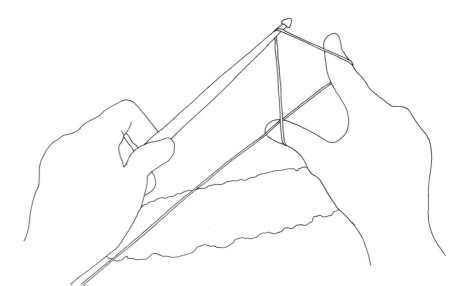

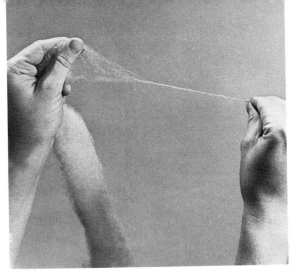

3.3　Finger spinning a starting length

3.5　Winding on the starting length

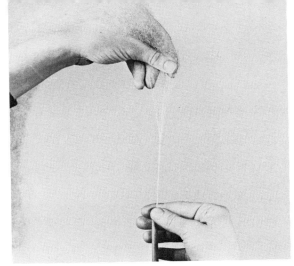

3.4　Spinning a starting length

3.6　After winding on the yarn is taken around the bottom of the spindle

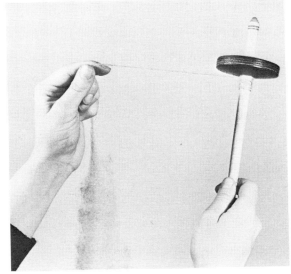

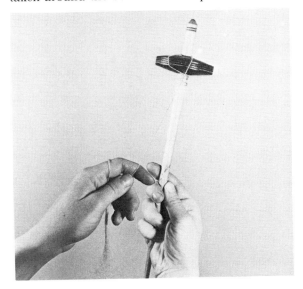

3.7　Making a half-hitch to secure the starting length (see diagram opposite)

3.8　Close-up of half-hitch

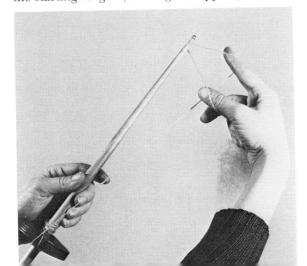

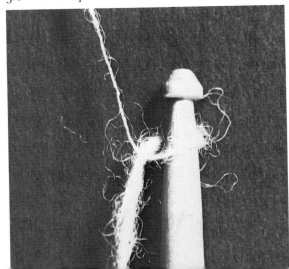

If a suitable length of yarn is available, that is, one of the same twist as the yarn to be spun and sufficiently hairy so that the new fibre supply has some spun fibres to grasp, the spinning of the starting length is unnecessary.

To join the starting length to the fibre supply:

Place about 10 cm (4 in) of the end of the spun yarn, which should still be hairy, into the fibre supply and hold this between the thumb and fingers of the left hand (fig. 3.9).

With the right hand start the spindle in a clockwise direction. This spin will cause a twist to run up the yarn and pull in the drafted fibres.

When the end of the fibre supply is twisted and joined to the previously spun yarn, pinch the twist with the

3.9 Joining the fibre supply to the starting length

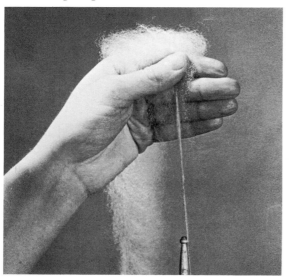

3.10 Drafting the fibres

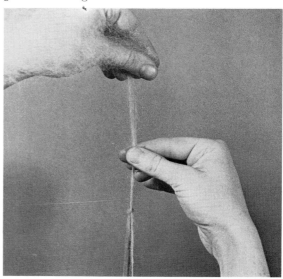

3.11 Drafting and guiding the twist

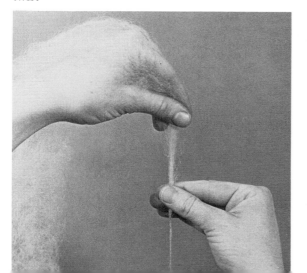

3.12 Winding on the spun yarn

thumb and index finger of the right hand to prevent it from travelling further into the supply.

Draft out the necessary fibres with the fingers of the left hand by pulling up or away from the right hand as previously described (fig. 3.10).

Pull out the fibre supply with the left-hand fingers and with the right-hand fingers release the squeeze on the twist up the yarn by sliding the fingers up the drafted fibres until they come close to the left-hand fingers guarding the supply (fig. 3.11). With practice this will become a continuous operation of drafting and sliding, while the spindle is kept rotating.

When the suspended length of spun yarn is too long to make the spindle easy to reach, it is time to wind on. Gather the spun length in the left hand and while holding it under tension wind on by turning the spindle in a clockwise direction and building up the cop, yarn package, so the weight is kept towards the whorl (fig. 3.12). Then wrap the remaining yarn under the whorl around the base of the stick, make a half-hitch at the tip to secure the length and begin again.

Remember that although there are three distinct divisions, fibre supply, drafting and twisting zone, there are only two processes, drafting and twisting, and that these are the purpose of the operations with the hands. The left hand holds the fibre supply and drafts out the fibres and the right hand controls the amount of twist and how it moves up the fibre supply.

Great wheel

Before beginning to spin on any wheel, it is important that it is in good working order. If it is an old wheel, make certain that the years of caked grease and dirt have been removed from the hub of the wheel so that it can run freely. Check also that the wheel and spindle are aligned, that the mountings are sturdy and the tensioning mechanism strong enough to perform its function. With the great wheel, which has the spindle horizontally mounted, it is important to make certain that the driving belt connecting the wheel to the spindle pulley is sufficiently taut so that there is no skipping or slipping to prevent the spindle from properly rotating. Check this tension before beginning. The belt should be a continuous band that has been spliced or sewn. Belt traction can be assisted by rubbing dressing on to the band. This dressing can be obtained from agricultural merchants and is used for obtaining greater friction on belt-driven machinery; alternatively the friction adhesives used for securing sanding discs to their bases can be used.

3.13   A great wheel
1 saddle
2 drive wheel
3 single drive belt
4 spindle head
5 tension adjustment

To use

Once tensioned, tie a length of spun yarn (Z twisted) on to the spindle. Turn the wheel in a clockwise direction sufficiently to take up several centimetres of the yarn. Then with a slightly attenuated rolag in the left hand, lie the spun length hanging from the spindle on top so that the fibre supply can be joined up (fig. 3.14). With the right hand on one of the spokes, begin to rotate the wheel clockwise, allowing the spun yarn to slip off the tip of the spindle in order to insert a twist. When sufficient twists have joined the starting length and fibre supply, draw off the fibres at an angle of approximately 135 degrees from the spindle.

The same three divisions and two processes apply as spinning with a spindle; there is a fibre supply, a drafting zone and twisting region. The left hand holds the fibre supply and drafts out the fibres between the fingers aided by the gentle tension of pulling off the spindle tip (fig. 3.15). The right hand turns the wheel at a constant speed while the slipping action of the spun yarn off the tip inserts the twist, and the shaking as it drops off the flat end of the spindle helps in drafting the fibres. If the spinner pulls too tightly on the tip or at the wrong angle the spindle rotation will cease.

3.14 Joining the fibre supply to the starting length

3.15 Drafting out the fibres

The thickness of the yarn is determined again by the drafting of the fibres. It is important that the drafting remains ahead of the twist to prevent the twist running up the undrafted supply. This is especially important as the right hand is no longer available to control the movement of the twist into the fibre supply. Having spun about a metre of yarn, reverse the wheel slightly by turning it in an anti-clockwise direction to unwind the yarn from the tip of the spindle; bring the left arm towards the wheel so that the newly spun yarn is at a 90 degree angle to the spindle and then wind on by turning the wheel clockwise once again. Build up the cop as illustrated (fig. 3.16), then the operation is ready to begin again. Yarn spun on the great wheel in this manner is Z twisted. Instructions for S twist can be found in chapter 6.

It is important with this technique, as with any other method of spinning, to develop a rhythm. The fingers of the left hand must learn to draft ahead of the twist so that the number of fibres drawn out is consistent. In drawing, spin to the same length each time before winding on so that the movements are smooth and consistent. Having filled the spindle, the cop if properly wound can simply be slipped off the spindle shaft for later use or skeining.

3.16 Winding on

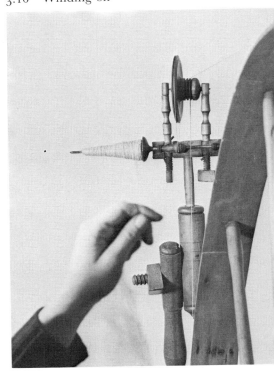

Treadle wheel

Numerous treadle wheels, diverse in style can be found today. Because of their common factor of a U-flyer, these wheels belong to the second group as previously described. This type of wheel is generally more widely known and became extremely popular, no doubt because it spun the fibres faster and with less effort. Twisting and winding can not only be done in one

3.17 A treadle wheel
1 saddle
2 treadle
3 footman
4 drive wheel
5 flyer and bobbin
6 doubled drive belt
7 mother of all
8 tension adjustment
9 distaff

3.18 An upright treadle wheel
1 treadle
2 drive wheel
3 tension adjustment
4 flyer and bobbin
5 doubled drive belt
6 distaff
7 flax cup

46

operation but the addition of a pedal (treadle) to activate the wheel frees the spinner's hands so both can be used for drafting fibres.

Although treadle wheels are diverse in their styling, they are for the most part of two varieties, the first having a doubled belt which drives both the flyer and the bobbin. The difference in diameter of the pulleys on the bobbin and flyer results in the bobbin turning faster than the flyer thus winding on the yarn as it rotates. Many wheels have multigrove pulleys, usually on the flyer, which give different ratios between winding and twisting. A high degree of twist with little winding is produced when the pulleys on bobbin and flyer are close in diameter, and when they have a large difference more winding with less twist is produced. The ratio of twist to winding is also altered by tension on the driving belt; the higher the tension the closer the mechanism will operate to the theoretical ratio of the diameter of the pulleys. Less tension allows the bobbin to slip when held back by the spun yarn and a more twisted yarn is produced. The spinning wheel is more sensitive to the demands of the spinner when the bobbin is allowed to slip and on old wheels it is often found that the diameter

3.19   A scotch-tension wheel
1 treadle
2 footman
3 drive wheel
4 flyer and bobbin
5 single drive belt
6 drive belt tension adjustment
7 bobbin drag adjustment

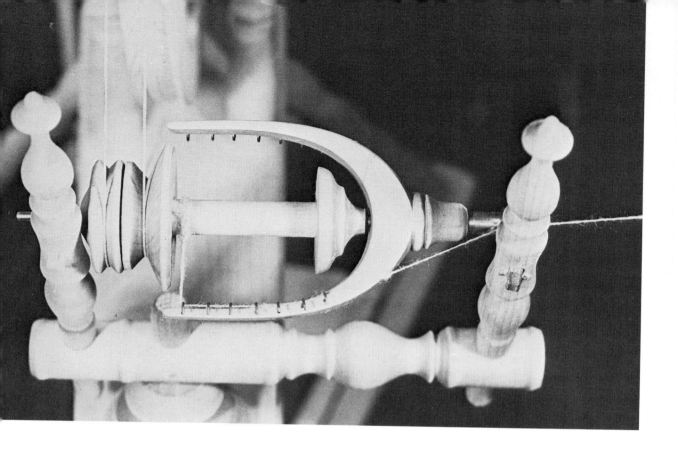

3.20 Tying on the starting length
to the bobbin

of the bobbin pulley has worn much smaller than intended. This diameter can easily be increased by tying a few turns of tightly spun yarn round the pulley to build it up to the desired diameter. This method is also useful on the non-adjustable wheels and provides a simple way of changing the wind/twist ratio. Worsted and strong hair fibres need a greater amount of twist which is sometimes difficult to achieve as most wheels are designed for woollen spinning. If the required amount of twist cannot be obtained by slackening the drive belt then it is advisable to build up the bobbin pulley and make it closer in diameter to that of the flyer.

The material for the driving belt should be chosen so that a good firm drive is obtained on the pulleys. This is obtained when it has a large area in contact with the pulley. Belts with diameters equal to or a little greater than the distance across the bottom of the pulley groove will give this. In using a belt with thickness as great as this, it is necessary to splice or sew the join otherwise a noticeable jolt occurs whenever the knot hits the pulley.

The second type of U-flyer wheel has a single driving belt from the wheel to a flyer and a separate tensioning

48

on the bobbin known as a scotch tensioning system or bobbin drag (fig. 3.19). With this type of mechanism, the bobbin is retarded by an adjustable brake and runs slower than the flyer which thus wraps the spun yarn on to the bobbin. Adjustment of the twist to winding ratio is made by changing the tension on the brake. The drive belt on this type of wheel should not slip as it drives the flyer, and a thick belt well seasoned with belt dressing should be used. Some wheels with a single belt can be converted to a double belt with a degree of satisfaction provided the pulley of the flyer and the one on the bobbin lie parallel to one another and in line with the drive wheel.

Regardless of the style of wheel, the same steps for spinning apply. The variations lie in the means of adjusting the tension for twisting and winding on and these are dealt with in the correction box at the end of the chapter.

To use

Not only are the wheels diverse in style but so are the techniques used for spinning. There is no right or wrong method; only some appear quicker, some easier to master and others are more adaptable for certain fibres. A spinner should select the one most suitable for the yarn being made and exploit it for that purpose. For ease of discussion, they can be described as long-draw or short-draw. To apply the basic principles of spinning to the treadle wheel, the short-draw will be the basic technique explained and the long-draw will be discussed under the heading of other techniques.

The short-draw provides a working basis for experimenting with the spinning of both woollen and worsted yarns, as well as fibres other than wool. For this reason it is proposed as a first method.

Following practice at treadling, begin by tying on to the bobbin approximately one metre of spun yarn. Turn the wheel in a clockwise direction until the bobbin takes up half this length.

Run the length over the hooks into the top and out through the eye of the orifice (fig. 3.20).
Attenuate one end of the fibre supply and with it in the left hand lay the end of the spun length across this supply holding it with the thumb (fig. 3.21). Turn the wheel in a clockwise direction and begin treadling slowly.
When the fibre supply is pieced to the spun length (fig. 3.22) the left hand begins and continues to draw out the fibres while the right hand guides the twist up these drafted fibres (fig. 3.23). This is a continuous operation, treadling going on at a steady pace whilst the left hand

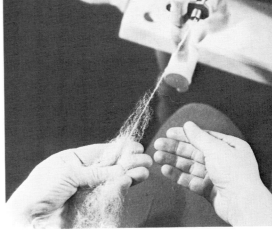

3.21 Joining the fibre supply to the starting length

3.22 Fibre supply is joined and the right fingers will now squeeze the spun yarn between the twist and drafting zone

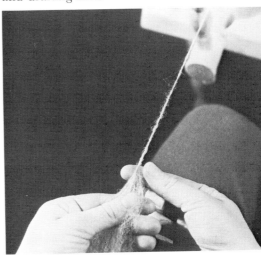

3.23 Drafting: short-draw technique

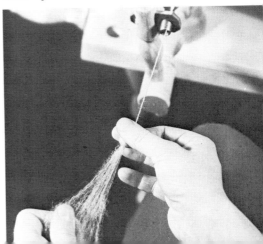

49

draws out the fibres to be twisted and the right hand controls the twist.

There are several points to remember. It is important that the hands sort the fibres faster than the feet treadle. The position of the hands varies very little, that is, the right hand remains in relatively the same position as the drafted fibres pass through the pinched thumb and index finger and emerge on the other side of these fingers as spun yarn while the left hand moves only as it drafts or 'pulls' back the fibre supply during drafting. It is important to let the wheel take the spun yarn for to hold back will result in overtwist or yarn breakage. Avoid the tendency to let the drafting come from the wheel or to pull fibres from the supply with the right-hand fingers which are solely used for guiding the twist. Also remember to move the yarn along each hook as spinning progresses, so that the bobbin is filled evenly. If the flyer has a row of hooks on each side, then work down one side, work back on the other row after re-threading through the top and eye of the orifice. A properly filled bobbin aids skeining and plying.

Correction box

Problem	Cause and Solution
Belt slipping	Requires more tension on the belt: adjust wood screw so that the mother of all moves further away from the drive wheel. Belt not tracking in grooves: thicker cord needed or an application of belt dressing required. Caused by a knot or badly joined belt catching: correct by splicing or sewing.
Belt jumping	Alignment between drive wheel and pulleys needs truing.
Wheel reversing direction	More treadling practice needed. Sometimes altering the placement of the treadling foot helps.
Treadling difficult	Too much tension on drive belt: release by moving the mother of all closer to the drive wheel. Poor adjustment on footman.
Difficulty in joining fibre supply	End of spun yarn not hairy enough to grip new supply: open end of yarn and attenuate fibre supply; hold the two securely until join is firm.
Difficulty in drafting	Poorly arranged fibres: better preparation needed. Twist entering the fibre supply: fingers not sorting fast enough.

Problem	Cause and Solution
Yarn not winding on	Not properly threaded: over bobbin, across hooks and through top and eye of orifice. Tangled on a hook or in the bobbin. Too thick for orifice. Not enough winding-on tension on doubled belt wheel: tighten belt by moving mother of all further away from driving wheel. On single belt, tighten the tension on the bobbin/scotch tensioner.
Too much pull on spun yarn or fibre supply	Too much tension: gradually lessen the tightness on the belt between the pulley and wheel on the doubled belt wheel and on the bobbin pulley for the scotch tension.
Fibres falling apart	Not enough twist: either treadle faster and hold back the yarn, or decrease the tension between the flyer pulley and drive wheel. Decrease tension on scotch brake.
Yarn snapping Overtwisted or kinked yarn	Too much twist: caused by holding on to the spun fibres too long and not letting it wind on at the adjusted speed. Correct by either treadling slower and drafting quicker, or increasing the tension between flyer pulley and drive wheel. Increase tension on scotch brake.
Thick and thin yarn formation	The result of not drafting the fibres consistently or in the short-draw intermittently releasing the pressure on the right hand finger-tips when guiding the twist.
Variation in the amount of twist	Irregular treadling. Pushing fibre supply towards orifice.

4 Experimenting

With other techniques

Although the basic principles of spinning are the same, the techniques can vary tremendously. It is advantageous, therefore, to experiment in developing techniques that are both comfortable and suitable to the type of yarn one wishes to produce within the scope of the fibres used. For this reason, a working knowledge of more than one technique may be useful.

Long-draw
For most design purposes, the short-draw provides a technique for spinning both woollen and worsted yarns and for dealing with various types and preparation of fibres. It offers an efficient method with the least number of movements, yet maximum control. However, another widely adopted method is the long-draw technique which is used throughout Britain. The drawing-in tension of the wheel is slightly reduced for this technique.

Start the wheel in a clockwise direction and with the fibre supply in the right hand (fig. 4.1), pinch the spun yarn with the left several centimetres from the orifice (fig. 4.2).
While twist accumulates in front of the left-hand fingers, draw the fibres out with the right hand across the body (fig. 4.3), while the left hand allows through only sufficient twist to give the attenuated fibre supply some strength.
When the fibre supply is comfortably or fully extended (an arm's length), release the hold of the left hand and allow additional twist to run up the drafted supply to make the completed yarn.
Ease the tension imposed by the right hand, swing the spun yarn in a more or less direct line towards the orifice and wind on to the bobbin (fig. 4.4).
With the new yarn fully wound on, both hands are close together and a few centimetres from the orifice. Keep a firm grip on the yarn with the thumb and index finger of the left hand until the twist from the wheel accumu-

4.1 Joining the fibre supply to the starting length: long-draw technique.

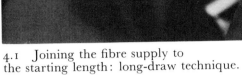

4.2 The left hand pinches the spun yarn several centimetres from the orifice

4.3 As the twist accumulates in front of the left-hand fingers, the right hand draws out the fibres

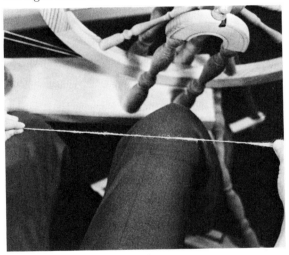

4.4 Winding on

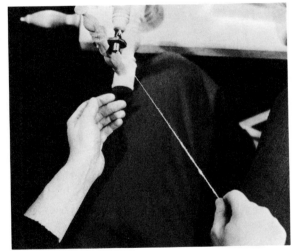

4.5 Twist accumulates and drafting begins again

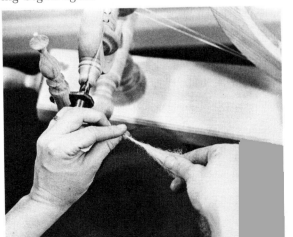

4.6 Position of the hands during drafting: long-draw technique.

lates (fig. 4.5), then repeat the drawing, twisting and winding on process.

Unlike the short-draw, where drafting, twisting and winding on is a continuous process, the long-draw is an intermittent process, and therefore it is essential that a rhythmic pattern of movements accompanied by a regular treadling be developed to assure consistency in the yarn produced.

With other fibres

The handspinner may come into contact with a wide variety of fibres that can be spun. These can be divided into two categories, natural and man-made. These categories can be further divided: natural fibres into animal, vegetable and mineral containing a wide range of ready-made fibrous forms produced by nature. The man-made fibres are divided according to the fibre-forming substances from which they are produced, either natural polymers or synthetics. The accompanying chart (fig. 4.7) is by no means a complete list of all the textile fibres, but it includes most of those available to handspinners.

4.7   Classification of textile fibres

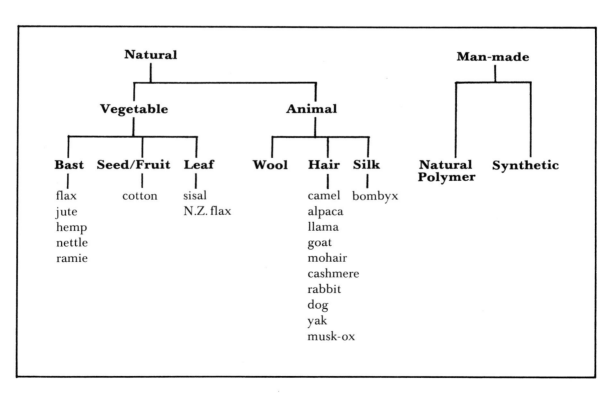

Natural fibres

The natural fibres vary widely amongst themselves, and for this reason, a knowledge of the characteristics of these fibres is useful if a spinner is to exploit their design potential.

Vegetable

It is widely believed that vegetable fibres were the first to be spun. Today, numerous plants are raised for their fibres and divide into three main groups. The first is the bast, or stem fibres, where the fibres are extracted from the fibrous bundles which form the inner bark. The second group is the fibre of seeds and fruits, and the third is the leaf fibres.

Bast Fibres
Flax: Of the bast fibres, flax, *Linum usitatissimum*, is the most popular with handspinners. As a fibre, it is believed to have been discovered in the prehistoric period and was widely used in the classical world. Its supremacy was broken with Arkwright's invention of a machine that would spin a cotton thread as strong as flax. It was not until the nineteenth century that the cultivation and preparation of it was to undergo industrialization.

One may wonder why a handspinner would undertake the laborious task of processing his own fibre when dressed flax is available relatively inexpensively. Not everyone has the acreage to raise his own sheep nor the conditions necessary for sericulture, but flax can easily be sown in the garden without commanding too much space or demanding too much attention during growing, yet gives the spinner the inexplicable satisfaction of spinning a fibre he has grown.

The species of flax are quite numerous and contemporary strains are now grown that can withstand the elements of rain and wind, yet grow to over a metre in height. The seeds are sown after the danger of frost has passed, traditionally on Good Friday. Since the object is to obtain good fibres, the seeds are sown fairly close to prevent branching, generally 2,500 to 3,000 plants per square metre. The plant takes about eight to fifteen days to germinate and eventually grows from $\frac{1}{2}$ to 1 m in height, having a thin spindle-shaped root, a stem branching at the top, smooth lanceolate leaves and, depending on the strain, a blue or white flower (fig. 4.8). The plant reaches maturity in 100 to 110 days and is ready for harvesting in late July or early August, when about two-thirds of the stem from the bottom up becomes yellow, and the seed capsules are turning from green to brown. If harvested later, when the plant and seeds are fully ripe, the fibres will be stiff and coarse. To preserve the full length of the fibres, the flax is pulled

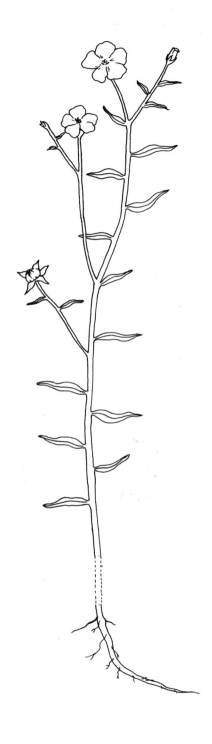

4.8 Flax (*Linum usitatissimum*)

4.9 To gain the maximum length of fibre, the flax is pulled out by the roots

4.10 Flax roots

4.11 Flax drying on the grass

4.12 Bundled flax drying under cover

out by the root (figs. 4.9, 10) instead of being cut, and is then left on the ground to dry for a few days.

After drying (figs. 4.11, 12), the plant is ready to be rippled, which consists of pulling the heads of the plant through a coarse comb called a hackle or rippler to remove the seed capsules (fig. 4.13). After rippling, the flax is 'retted', a term derived from 'rotting'. It is a process which decomposes the adhesive substances that bind the bast fibres to each other and also the woody inner portion of the stem (fig. 4.14). There are several modes of retting flax apart from the chemical process used by industry; these include running-water retting, dam or stagnant-water retting and dew retting. Since the latter is the most practical method for home production, only a brief account of the others is necessary. Running-water retting involves the flax being bundled and then packed into wooden crates lined with straw. The crates are weighted with stones to anchor them a few inches below the water. The length of time necessary for retting is dependent on the quantity of flax and the temperature of the water. Retting in running water usually requires ten to twenty days. Retting is completed, in this method as well as any other, when the central woody portions spring up from the fibrous sheath.

Retting in stagnant water is much quicker than in running water, because the organic matter in the water aids the fermentation process. The bundles of flax are steeped in ponds where there is a suitable arrangement for admitting and discharging water. Retting in this manner requires careful observation because of the dangers of over-retting, that is, fermentation taking place too quickly and frequently irregularly, which can destroy or weaken the fibre. Following the removal of the flax from the water, it is then drained and thinly spread out on a field, where it is occasionally turned and left for a week or more. This is known as grassing in which the action of dew, air, rain and sunlight completes the removal of the adhesive substances in the flax. Dew retting requires little more than this spreading or grassing. It is the easiest and safest method

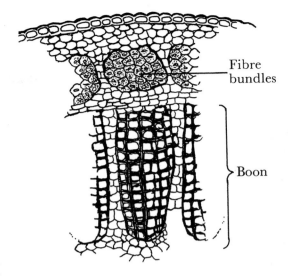

4.14   Flax cross-section

Fibre bundles

Boon

4.15   Flax dew-retting

4.13   Rippling to remove seed pods

4.16 Breaking the retted flax

4.17 Breaking the inner stem to free the fibre

4.18 Scutching to remove the remaining boon

4.19 Ruffling with the coarsest hackle

for the home producer to employ. The flax is simply spread thinly on the grass and subjected to the action of the weather for six to eight weeks (fig. 4.15). Since moisture aids fermentation, damp (British) weather is ideal. A good grassing area is under trees because they hold the morning dew. To prevent the flax from drying out, the fibres can be moistened by using a watering can. After several weeks of exposure, check the fibres to see if they have rotted sufficiently. When retting is complete, rake the flax from the grass, secure in bundles and place in loose stooks until dry.

The colour of the flax is determined by the method of retting; a honey-cream colour is the result of water retting while dew-retted fibres are generally grey or darker brown. After retting, the flax is dried and is then ready for the next operation, which is known as breaking.

The aim of this operation is to break the brittle, woody centre of the flax stem while leaving the fibres unharmed. This is accomplished by placing a bundle of flax across the bars of a flax break and banging the knife down with considerable force (figs. 4.16, 17). In place of a break, a wooden mallet of some sort can be used to break the fibre against a board. The final step in the breaking operation, which is known as swingling or scutching, consists of beating the flax against a board with a wooden knife until all the broken boon falls away and leaves the fibre on its own (fig. 4.18). The flax is now stored in bundles until it is ready for the final cleaning, a process called hackling.

The object of hackling is the further separation of the fibres by combing. Dampen the bundles slightly and hold at one end while drawing through the teeth of the hackle. Repeat the operation of drawing the fibres until they are straightened and the short bits removed. Then repeat the process at the other end of the bundle. The first hackle is called a ruffler (fig. 4.19). The process produces two types of fibres, the short tangled fibres called tow and the long fibres called line (fig. 4.20). The line is stored in a bundle called a strick or queue for spinning later, and the tow (formerly twisted into rope for home use) is now used for spinning into a coarse yarn. Give the queue a final fine combing after removing from storage before dressing on a distaff.

The dressing of the distaff further prepares the line for spinning by providing a continuous fibre supply. Several pieces of equipment should be gathered before starting. These are: a length of string long enough to go about the preparer's waist with a few centimetres to spare, an apron or tea towel, about two metres of ribbon, a distaff and tissue paper for the padding of the distaff if it is not a lantern type. For a wheel without a distaff, a

4.20 The short tow separated from the flax line by further hackling

4.21 Tying the strick to the waist

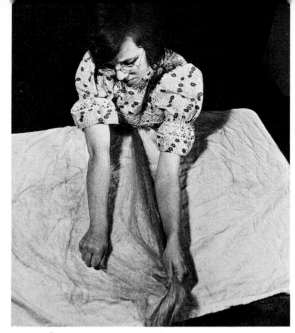

4.22 Spreading the line for the distaff

broom handle or collapsed umbrella swift lashed to a chair can be used. Remove about 50 grams (1½ oz) of line from the strick. Hold it by one end and shake it to open the fibres. If necessary, open the end by working it through a fine hackle.

Knot one end of the strick securely in front of the dresser (fig. 4.21). Many spinners work in an armless chair and arrange the flax on an apron across the lap. However, others find it easier to tie the flax to their waist and work on a cloth at a table.

4.23 Direction of spreading reversed

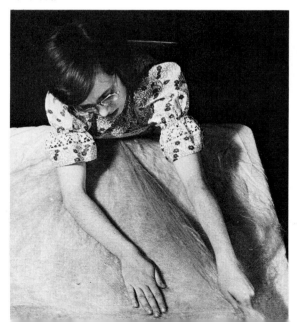

4.24 Building up criss-crossed layers of fibre

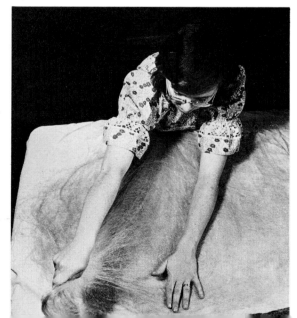

4.25 Distaff in position prior to dressing

4.26 Rolling the fibres around the distaff

4.27 Securing the dressed line with a ribbon

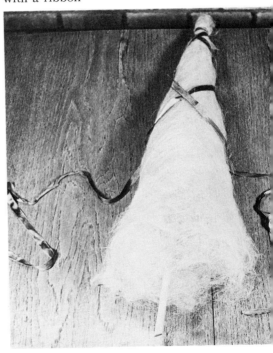

Having shaken and tied the flax, take the strick in the left hand and keep it stretched and tensioned. With the right hand, begin to pull a few fibres away from the strick (fig. 4.22). The palm is sometimes helpful in this fanning and layering operation. Working towards the left, continue this fanning operation, taking care that none of the fibres lie in a straight line from the tied point. Having fanned out to the left, take the strick in the right hand and work back towards the right, this time with the left hand and fingers layering the fibres in a criss-cross manner (fig. 4.23).

Continue to layer the fibres in this manner, working back and forth until all the fibres are arranged so that they lie criss-cross in a fine light web (fig. 4.24).

Cut the tie at the waist and remove the string. Tidy any stray fibres by tucking them into the criss-cross web. If necessary pad the distaff and lay it at one end of the fanned fibres (fig. 4.25).

Slowly roll the distaff across the fibres, making certain that the top of the distaff is kept in conjunction with the top of the arranged fibres (fig. 4.26).

Carefully pat the meeting point. Tuck away any of the stray ends at the bottom of the distaff into the body of the fibres.

Fasten the flax to the top of the distaff with a secure single knot made in the middle of the ribbon and cross the two ends around the flax before securing the ribbon with a bow at the base of the fibres (fig. 4.27). Open out the ends at the top of the distaff.

In early Colonial America, it was traditional to secure the dressed flax with a ribbon, the colour of which depended on the marital status of the spinner, green for a married woman and red for a maiden. With the distaff dressed the flax is ready to be spun by drawing it from the continuous supply.

The technique for spinning flax is different from that used for wool because it requires moisture and a roll and squeeze operation, and also because it is usually S twisted as this is the natural twist that the fibre responds to in nature when wet. The fibre can be moistened with either water or a flax jelly made by boiling about a teaspoon of flax seeds in a cup of water. Many old wheels have tin or pewter cups attached to them in which the spinner would dip his fingers to keep them damp for the proper spinning of the flax.

Apart from the necessity of moistening the fingers for the ease of spinning, the actual technique for drawing and spinning the fibres is different. In Britain, many spinners employ a one-handed method where the flax fibres are drawn down from the distaff by the fingers of the left hand which help also to 'roll in' a twist by rubbing the fibres between the tips of the fingers and thumb. The drawing, twisting and winding on are a continuous operation and the wheel is treadled in an anti-clockwise direction. It can be advantageous to employ both hands, the left to draw down the fibres from the distaff, and the moistened fingers of the right to guide the twist up the drawn fibres by rolling and squeezing the fibres to be twisted between the fingers and thumb (fig. 4.28). This technique of drawing with the left hand and twisting with the right is also a continuous operation with the winding on taking place at the speed at which it is drawn into the bobbin. If the distaff has been properly dressed, the only need for stopping the wheel is to adjust the filling of the bobbin.

The method chosen for spinning tow depends on the length of the fibres. Longer fibres can be combed and drawn into a roving, and short irregular lengths can be spun directly from a handful of the teased fibres. As the tow is much drier than flax the use of flax jelly on the fingers greatly assists spinning.

The spun linen can be softened by boiling in soapy water and rubbing it several times. To bleach the skeins, the safest method is to moisten the skeins in warm water and hang out in the sunshine. The time needed depends on the amount of sunshine.

Most spinners find it easiest to bleach the article after it has been made. Again the safest method is grassing, because, although a rather slow process, the results are permanent. It involves no more than laying the material on the grass for some weeks while the oxygen in the air, as

4.29   Jute (*Corchorus* species)

4.30   Hemp (*Cannabis sativa*)

well as that given off from the surrounding plants, attacks and destroys the colour particles in the fibre until the linen is finally white.

The process can be hastened by boiling equal weights of soap and soda (250 grams or 8 oz) in water (4 litres or 1 US gallon). After cooling slightly, add the moistened linen and boil in this mixture for about two hours making certain that the linen is well covered with water at all times. Then expose the linen, which is kept moistened, to oxygen and sun for three days and the combination of boiling and natural bleaching is repeated several times until the coloured particles are destroyed.

Jute: Jute fibres come from the inner bark of the plant, *Corchorus capsularis* and *olitorius*, which is believed to have originated in the Mediterranean region. The plants, which grow to a height of as much as 5 m (16 ft) with a stem diameter of 2 cm (0.75 in) produce as much as five times the quantity of fibre as flax per stem. It is second only to cotton in annual production. As a herbaceous annual, the plant is frequently harvested with a hand sickle. It is processed in a manner similar to flax.

The strands of the fibre vary considerably in colour, degree of lustre and coarseness. Because of the varying coarseness and long length of the strands, the fibres cannot be easily dressed on a distaff in the manner previously described for flax. Jute, when purchased in hanks for spinning usually has cut ends where the fibre length has been chopped. Take a small quantity from the hank, about 30 grams (1 oz), and as with the flax, hold one end while shaking the fibres free at the other. If the fibres do not separate, hold the bundle in the middle and comb open each end of the fibres. Separate into smaller bundles or rovings of jute and spin by a worsted technique using olive-oil emulsion to moisten the fingers (see Chapter 2). Jute yarn is more hairy than flax and moisture can cause it to disintegrate. It does not bleach easily, in fact, it has a tendency to turn brown in prolonged exposure to sunlight. However, it does have an affinity for chemical dyes.

Hemp: Hemp is another bast fibre and similar to jute. Known in ancient China, there are several varieties of plant, although the species *Cannabis sativa* is the annual primarily grown for cordage. Widely cultivated, it grows from 2 to 4 m (7 to 13 ft) in height. It is processed in a manner similar to flax, but resembles jute, although able to withstand water better, and because of its strength and durability is best suited for making string. There are other varieties of bast fibres, similar to hemp and jute, known as sunn or sann, also referred to as Indian or Bomba Kemp and kennaf which is called Guinea

66

Hemp. The spinning of hemp is similar to jute, although the quality available is usually poorer and, therefore, difficult and unpleasant to manage. It is interesting to note that this same plant, which has been cultivated from 28 BC in China, was taken to America by the early settlers as a source of blue or violet dye. The dried leaves of this plant, more commonly known as marijuana, are sometimes smoked.

Nettles: There are several varieties of nettles grown for their fibres. These include species of the family *Urticaceae*. The stems are processed similarly to flax and produce soft cream or grey fibres which are as much as 1 m in length and a hardwearing yarn can be spun from them.

Ramie belongs to a family of stingless nettles. It is known as Rhea when from the species *Boehmeria tenacissema* which grows in tropical countries, or China grass when from the species *B. nivea* which is cultivated in temperate climates. The plant, a perennial, grows to a height of 1 to 2 m. It is harvested when the stalks turn yellow. Ramie cannot be retted like the other bast fibres so a process known as decortication is employed. Decortication processes vary, but it is a way of peeling the fibre from the stalk. The fibres must also be degummed by using either a soaking and scraping method, or by boiling in caustic alkali solution. The fibre itself is white, lustrous and silken in appearance, a cross between prepared mohair and white silk. It is available commercially prepared and comes in rovings that are best spun by a worsted method. The spun thread lacks elasticity, but is strong.

Seed and fruit fibres

Another source of fibres is the hairy substances that surround the seeds or fruit of certain plants. These include kapok (*Ceiba pentandra*), tree cotton (*Bombax ceiba*), milkweed (*Asclepias* species) and cotton (*Gossypium* species) which is the major commercial vegetable fibre today.

Cotton: The fibre is the soft down hair attached to the seeds of plants of the mallow family. There is a wide variety of cotton, but most of the quality species are annuals reaching heights of 1 to 2 m. Sown in the spring, the plant produces many creamy coloured blossoms that soon turn pink, drop by the third day and die to leave a small green pad or boll. The boll contains seeds and it is on these seeds that the cotton fibres in the form of hairy down begin to grow, for its purpose in nature is to gather moisture for the seed. The boll continues to ripen and the hairs to grow until, after about fifty days, the boll bursts to reveal a downy mass of fibres. The bolls are

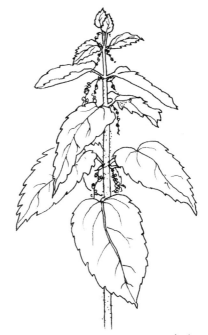

4.31   Nettle (*Urticaceae* species)

4.32   Cotton (*Gossypium* species) (top left to right): ripe boll, seeds, ginned cotton, cotton rolag.

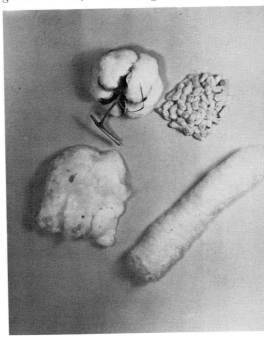

67

harvested in the autumn and then ginned, a mechanical process which separates the fibres from the seeds. Only a few handspinners are fortunate enough to have access to newly harvested bolls, so that they can gin their own cotton. Most cotton reaches spinners separated from the seed. The varieties vary and the top quality, with a fibre length from 2.5 to 3.5 cm (1 to 1.4 in), is Sea Island, Egyptian or American–Egyptian. The next quality includes American Uplands with staple 2 to 2.5 cm. (0.8 to 1 in). These are the qualities best suited to hand-spinning. When buying cotton, look for a fine bright staple of reasonable length and freedom from impurities, such as dirt or chaff. As with other fibres, cotton is easier to manage if arranged prior to spinning. After ginning, the fibres are compressed into bales and as a result they are often matted and pressed together. They are much easier to manage when fluffed out. This can be accomplished in several ways; they can be steamed or whipped with a flexible stick or bow, but the easiest method is carding. This should be done with carders having longer, finer and closer-set teeth than those used for wool carding. Once fluffed, the cotton is ready for spinning. Each region where cotton is grown has a traditional way of spinning the fibre. Where a spindle is employed, the fibres are often spun with the spindle rotating in a shell or dish, so that there is no weight on the suspended fibres. In southern America, the slaves spun cotton on the plantation's great wheel. In India cotton was spun on the charkha.

The difficulty with spinning cotton, or any short staple fibre, is the short quick draw that must be employed. It is necessary to draw out the fibres in a short fan-like arrangement with a smaller drafting zone, than used when spinning wool. The technique for spinning these shorter fibres on a wheel is aided for some spinners by working closer to the orifice while fanning the fibres out, using a twisting movement with the drafting hand to help the drawing out. It is also important to adjust the wheel so that the winding on speed is reduced, but still maintain a high amount of twist to give the yarn strength.

Leaf fibres

Sisal (*Agave sisalana*), henequen (*Agave fourcroydes*), and New Zealand flax (*Phormium tenax*) belong to the leaf fibre family. They are much coarser than the other vegetable fibres in the bast or seed groups. Native to New Zealand this latter plant produces long stiff swordlike leaves which grow up to 2.5 m in length and from which the fibres are obtained. After preparation it is spun the same way as other coarse vegetable line, requiring dampening while spinning.

4.33 New Zealand flax
(*Phormium tenax*)

68

Animal

Animal fibres come chiefly from domesticated animals, although in terms of commercial production they represent only a small percentage of textile fibres produced annually. Besides being readily accessible, their unique qualities offer a wide design potential to the handspinner. Fibres of animal origin can be grouped as wool, hair and silk. The term wool can be confusing, but used on its own it means the fibrous covering of sheep. The characteristics and spinning techniques for wool are discussed in Chapters 2 and 3. The fibrous covering of other animals is termed hair. However, some animals, such as the camel and cashmere goat, produce two types of fibres, a coarse outer coat known as hair and a soft downy undercoat which is termed wool. To distinguish it from the animal's coat as well as from wool produced by sheep, it is usually provided with the name of the animal, that is, camel wool, cashmere wool.

Hair
This group is extremely large since it includes all fibre-bearing animals from the yak to the angora rabbit. Although related by a similar chemical structure, they vary considerably in their length, fineness, texture and handle, all of which influences their use.

Camel: The bactrian, or two-humped species, of northern China and Mongolia is considered to produce the best camel fibres. The animal sheds about two kilograms of hair annually. The hair which falls in clumps varies in quality. There is the coarse outer coat of wiry hair that ranges from 10 to 25 cm (4 to 10 in) in length, and from reddish brown to brownish black. This is the third quality which commercially is separated by combing from the first quality of the soft downy undercoat. The fine undercoat is a tannish colour with fibres averaging about 6 to 8 cm (2.4 to 3 in). Second quality camel contains a mixture of the coarse, wiry outer hairs and downy undercoat.

All three qualities are obtainable for handspinning. The outer hair, which is combed from the undercoat, is available usually in roving form. It is best spun by a worsted technique. Because hair fibres lack the adhering qualities of sheep's wool they also require more twist. Some spinners find it advantageous to oil their fingers with olive oil when dealing with dry scoured hairs.

The downy undercoat is prepared by carding. If the spinner has second quality camel hair, the coarse outer hairs can be picked out from the downy under-coat. Tease over the fibres to open any matted section, then card in the usual manner. Because of the length of

4·34 Camel

69

the fibres, they are easier to manage if spun by a short-draw method. If the fibres are too dry to handle easily then, after a first teasing, sprinkle lightly with olive-oil emulsion which should then be blended through the fibres before starting to card. It is advantageous if designing a hardwearing yarn for fabric to blend (see Chapter 6) the downy hair with a suitable wool which has the essential felting and wearing qualities desired, which the camel undercoat lacks. Camel hair is attacked by moths and acids in a manner similar to wool.

Alpaca, llama, vicuna: New World descendants of the camel are the alpaca and its relatives, the llama and vicuna. They are raised with the exception of the vicuna throughout southern Peru, northern Argentina and Bolivia. The alpaca stands about 1 m high at its shoulder. It yields approximately 2.5 kilograms (6 lb) of hair each year with a staple as long as 60 cm (2 ft). The fibres are sheared and sorted into seven grades. They range in colour from black to white including shades of brown and can be prepared by either carding or combing and spun similarly to wool.

Llama hair can be dealt with in the same way as alpaca. The soft undercoat of the llama resembles the hair of the alpaca whereas the outercoat is coarser. Every two years the animal yields approximately 2.5 kilograms (6 lb) of hair with a staple length between 14 and 28 cm (5.5 and 11 in). The colours include white, grey, black and shades of brown. Llama and alpaca hair is equivalent in fineness to a 55–60s quality wool, whereas that of the vicuna is in the range of 120–130s. One of the finest fibres, it is no longer available as the wild animal must be killed before it is obtained.

Goat: There are wide varieties of goat hair suitable for handspinning, apart from the wiry hairs of the common meadow goat, including the hair from the angora and cashmere goats.

Angora goat is the source of mohair and is reared in South Africa and the United States, as well as Turkey, its original breeding place. Angora goat is longer, finer and silkier than that of other goats. The length of the fibre varies from 10 cm (4 in) to as much as 30 cm (12 in), depending on the shearing schedule. An angora kid at six months will have fibres from 10 to 14 cm (4 to 5.5 in); a full year's growth will give a staple length from 20 to 30 cm (8 to 12 in), while a clipping twice a year, which is the practice in California and Texas, means, of course, a staple of half the yearly growth. The animal can provide as much as 2.5 kilograms (6 lb) of mohair at each clipping. As with any fibre-producing animal, the quality of its coat varies, natural and vege-

4.35 Alpaca

table impurities accounting for at least a third of its weight. Grading is into three categories: the first being tight lock which has very fine ringlets; the second, flat lock which includes wavy fibres of medium quality and the third is fluffy open fleece.

The handspinner will find that mohair fibres, apart from being stronger than wool, are silky and lustrous in texture. They also respond well to dyeing. Mohair is available in prepared combed top which is best split to aid drafting. A worsted technique is used for spinning with a high degree of twist. Mohair is also obtainable in the grease and can be either worsted prepared and spun or blended with wool, carded and woollen spun.

Cashmere is the fine soft undercoat of the Cashmere goat which is raised in northern Italy, Tibet, Iran, Afghanistan and parts of China. In the spring, the downy undercoat is combed from this domesticated animal's coat. Commercially the hair fibres are combed again to further separate the coarse outer hairs which are 8.5 to 10 cm (3.3 to 4 in) long from the soft and extremely fine cashmere wool which is a fibre about 2.5 to 8.5 cm (1 to 3.3 in) long. The fibre is extremely expensive because each goat produces little more than 125 grams (4.5 oz) of this down annually which is either grey, buff coloured or white.

The cashmere available commercially to the handspinner usually has most of the coarse hairs removed; if they are present, they can be removed by picking them out. These coarse hairs can be blended with wool by carding although the spun yarn has no desirable properties. The soft undercoat can then either be carded in a manner used for any fine downy wool or spun directly from a handful of the fibres. The technique of spinning from a handful of teased fibres can be employed with other short staple fibres such as cotton, camel and angora rabbit. Spinning technique is a matter of preference although the short draw permits a better control over drafting and must be used if spinning short stapled fibres from a teased handful. Cashmere lends itself to a soft lightly twisted yarn.

Yak: Yak is bred in central Asia and Tibet and belongs to the ox family. The grey to black hair fibres gathered from this large animal average 8 to 14 cm (3 to 5.5 in) and are softer and less wiry than some goat species. It is also available combed which when spun by a worsted method requires considerable twist. The spun yarn is coarse and crude.

Musk ox: The musk-ox is native to Canada and Greenland and is more closely related to sheep than to true oxen. It develops a heavy coat which consists of a dense

4.36   Cashmere Goat

4.37   Yak

4.38   Musk-ox

soft wool similar to but longer stapled and coarser than cashmere overlaid by thick guard hairs that reach to the ground. The undercoat is shed in the spring and can be teased or picked to remove the guard hair and then spun in the same way as cashmere.

Dog hairs: A variety of dog hairs can be used for spinning, but they are relatively difficult to control because of their texture. Heavier and woollier hairs are easier to control but it is advantageous to use oil prior to carding. Dog hairs are best managed when blended (see Chapter 6) with wool in the grease. This blending facilitates spinning and aids the strength of the spun yarn.

4.39 Rabbit

Angora rabbit: Angora rabbit is another fibre-producing animal. Its soft hairy coat of fur is rooed or clipped as often as every three months and annually this can amount to 250 to 500 grams (9 to 18 oz) of fibre. The fibre is of two types: long hairy outercoat and a soft fine under fur. If the angora fur has been obtained by combing it may require blending with wool if the fibres are too short, or carded in a manner similar to cotton and other short-stapled fibres to release and open the matted tangled hair. Rooed or clipped fur can have the ends opened by teasing with the fingers or by lightly pulling through the end teeth of a carder. The handling of the teased fibres is aided by sprinkling them lightly with talcum powder. Spinning is by a short-draw or worsted technique to facilitate control. Spun yarn from angora rabbit washes and felts in a manner similar to wool; its softness lends itself to use for knitting or crochet.

Silk: Silk is an unusual fibre produced by the silkworm caterpillar, *Bombyx mori.* In order to protect itself during metamorphosis from caterpillar to moth the insect in spinning a cocoon produces the only finished thread in nature. It emerges as a moth from this cocoon when ready to mate by softening one end of the cocoon with a liquid secretion. To collect raw silk, the chrysalis is killed by dry heat before it emerges from the cocoon. The cocoon is then boiled to remove the gum covering, sericin, and then is carefully unreeled as a monofilament classified as raw silk. The silk available to handspinners is the waste made during the production of raw silk and is termed waste silk. It can arise from several sources. The first source of waste silk is from the thread produced by the silkworm to secure itself to a solid object, such as straw, on which it develops in its cocoon. Known as blaze, it is the least lustrous fibre, filled with sericin. Another form of waste is from the pierced cocoon, where the moth has been permitted to emerge for breeding or

72

that from damaged cocoons. Waste is also obtained from the first reeling or unwinding which in Britain is termed knubbs. Another source of filature waste consists of the inner casing that surrounds the dead chrysalis, called basin waste.

The silk filaments, prior to spinning, must be degummed. Degumming involves removing the sericin by boiling the silk in soapy water. In preparing the degumming bath, remember that silk is attacked by alkali. The first bath should contain water and soap flakes in the ratio of three litres ($\frac{3}{4}$ US gallon) to 30 grams (1 oz) and the silk should be simmered for as long as two hours. If gum remains, a subsequent bath containing less soap flakes should be employed. Once the gum has been dissolved, the silk should be rinsed clear and left to dry. The waste silk can then be carded to align the fibres in the same manner as any short fibre. The prepared waste can then be spun on the wheel using a short draw, but account must be taken of the weak nature of the fibres and they must be spun under less tension. Spinning with a supported spindle, either on a table or in a dish, is another technique that can be used.

Tussah silk is produced by other species of silkworms living 'wild' and can be yellow, buff or grey. Both cultivated and tussah silk waste is available prepared in either laps or slivers. The laps resemble a gauze-like material and can be combed and drawn into a roving for spinning. Slivers are tops of silk waste which should be handled as any combed arrangement. The spun yarn and eventually the finished articles should be laundered in soap flakes, rinsed thoroughly in soft water and dried gently; they can be dyed. Articles from cultivated silkworms should be ironed under moderate heat with a cloth while damp, although tussah silk articles are best ironed when dry.

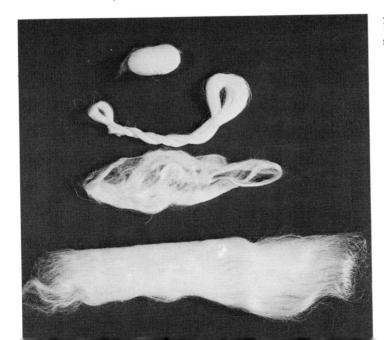

4.40 Silk (*Bombyx mori*) (top to bottom): cocoon, raw silk, waste silk, silk sliver.

Man-made fibres

With an increasing number of man-made fibres on the market, many handspinners are exploring the use of these fibres. Man-made fibres are produced by extruding natural polymers and synthetic substances in liquid form through fine jets called spinnerets. On emerging from the spinneret, the liquid solidifies to form a fine filament. There is no technical limit to the length of the filament produced and yarn can be produced by lightly twisting these continuous filaments as they are extruded to form a compact smooth yarn. The limitations of the continuous filament yarn are obvious so it is usually converted into a top resembling natural fibres and then spun in the conventional manner. Man-made fibres of interest to the handspinner are of the latter type. The way in which the continuous filament, called tow, is converted can greatly change the nature of the resulting fibre. A worsted top is produced when the tow is stretched and heated between rollers which break the continuous filaments into random lengths resulting in a fibre supply having staple fibres lying fairly parallel to each other. This stretching at high temperature produces an interesting effect on acrylic fibres: on cooling they retain their stretched length but revert to their original size on reheating, shrinking by as much as 30%. Usually this type of fibre is fully relaxed during the conversion process but sometimes it is blended with a non-shrinking fibre and then spun. The yarn is then subjected to boiling water and the unrelaxed fibres revert to their original length, causing the yarn to shorten and increase in bulk. Most interesting effects can be produced by this type of fibre but care should be taken that they are not inadvertently included where their properties would be detrimental to the completed project.

In spinning man-made materials the size of the drafting zone is determined by the staple length as with natural fibres, but as these fibres are usually very strong it is most important that the twist is not allowed to run into the fibre supply, where a thick knot of fibres impossible to draft or break can quickly become produced.

Instructions for burning tests

In doing the test, make sure that a reasonable bulk of fibre is introduced into the flame and not just stray individual fibres which will nearly always burn easily. On removing the fibres from the flame, observe if they continue burning or extinguish themselves. Remember that most prepared fibres have had oil added for easing in combing and this may be sufficient to maintain combustion in some cases. If an animal fibre is suspected, observe the smell of hair. The group of man-made fibres consisting of the thermo-plastics will all melt when samples are brought near to a flame. No natural or rayon fibres melt in this way.

74

Burning tests

	ODOUR	MANNER	REMAINS	FIBRE
SELF-EXTINGUISHING	burnt hair	rapidly with loud crackling	charred tangled mass	cow horse-hair goat
		quickly with sizzling smoke on removal from flame	crisp black inflated mass	yak karakul alpaca camel hair camel down cashmere tussah silk
			black bead-like inflated mass	wool
	burnt grass	crackles	grey ash	manila
	fresh celery	shrinks from flame, burns with a hissing	hard round fawn coloured bead	nylon
NOT SELF-EXTINGUISHING	burnt hair	rapidly with sizzling	black mass	gummed silk
	burnt paper		grey or black ash	raw cotton kapok retted flax
		steadily	no ash	bleached cotton mercerized cotton linen viscose rayon cuprammonium rayon
			smouldering ash	jute ramie
		fairly quickly	white ash	hemp sisal
	burnt flesh	softens, melts, ignites to smokey flame	round crisp bead	orlon courtelle acrilan polyacrilonitrile fibres

5 Natural dyeing

Alkanet (*Alkanna* or *Anchusa tinctoria*)

This art is so useful and the practice of it at the same time so entertaining . . . when once a lady has perfected one colour, she will not rest satisfied till she has acquired a further knowledge of colours in general.

William Tucker (*The Family Dyer and Scourer* 1831)

Dyeing, like spinning, is an ageless art. In every civilization, from remote ages to the present day, the art of dyeing has been carried on, playing an important part in adding beauty to the everyday world. Chinese history records dyeing as early as 3,000 BC, yet the first evidence of the art in western civilization is with the Swiss Lake-Dwellers, 2,000 BC.

Dye techniques improved slowly, predominately by trial and error, until the eighteenth century, when European and American industrial dyers, influenced by the French, began to employ a scientific approach. The manufacture of the first chemical dye in 1856 brought the rapid rise of a synthetic dye industry throughout Europe, decreasing the economic importance of natural dyestuffs.

The development of textile dyeing and trade routes provides very interesting reading, although beyond the scope of this book. For the craftsman interested in the use of natural dyestuffs, the reproduced papers and manuscripts of early textile dyers and, in particular, of the American colonists and their descendants, provide informative material, for, as in the case of spinning, dyeing was also carried out in the home. A lack of funds, and in many instances the unobtainability of luxury dyes known in Europe, made households dependent on their natural surroundings for dyes. Trial and error gave rise to local recipes which were passed from generation to generation.

How often the question is raised, why natural dyes? Natural dyeing is time consuming, to an extent messy, and occasionally a failure compared to chemical dyeing which is quick, effective and relatively colourfast and failure proof. So why bother? Not until one has searched for and found, gathered, prepared and finally lifted wool from a pot of simmering natural dye, will one know why a dyer looks at nature and her colour-giving landscape in an exciting way. For this reason, an introductory handbook on the craft of handspinning would not be complete without working methods for the natural dyeing of fleece and handspun, because of the possibilities for yarn design that it offers. The aim is to supply working methods for experimenting with natural dyes and provide a link between dyeing and handspinning.

Preparation for dyeing

In dyeing with natural materials, a few moments devoted to preparation and adherence to basic procedure are well spent to assure success.

Equipment
A certain amount of equipment is required for dyeing which should be used for this purpose only. Before beginning the following items should be organized:

Dye pot: This should be selected with care. First it should be large but still manageable. Next, it should be made of suitable material: iron, copper and brass should not be used. Stainless steel or unchipped enamelled ware can both be easily maintained and are relatively unreactive chemically. Ideally, several vessels, one used just for mordanting, another for dyeing and a third, smaller one, for samples, are most practical. Several preserving jars are also useful for simmering small test samples. Indigo requires a separate vessel, and many dyers prefer the use of a glass one, so the dye can be observed and because the chemicals used are highly reactive.

Scales: These are necessary for weighing the fibres and quantities of dyestuffs and chemicals. A dietary or letter scale is useful for small quantities and ordinary kitchen scales are handy for fibres or fresh dyestuffs which can be contained in a polythene bag while weighing.

Thermometer: A cooking thermometer which clamps on to a pan is ideal; this is particularly necessary for indigo where the temperature is critical.

Measuring jug: A heatproof glass (Pyrex) one is easy to maintain and can withstand hot liquids; it should have measurement graduations.

Bedstraw (*Galium verum*)

77

Spoons: Since these are used to measure chemicals, non-metallic or stainless steel are best.

Stirring rods: Glass rods are recommended, but are expensive. Small wooden dowels are a good substitute.

Mordanting agents: These are discussed later in the chapter.

Water: The importance of water is frequently overlooked; dyers should use soft water, as hard water can be injurious to wool and ruin the brilliance of the colours. Rain water provides a readily available supply of soft water; it can be collected and stored for later use.

Other equipment: Rubber gloves, muslin bags, rinsing buckets, tongs, labels and a pencil are useful.

Collecting and preparing materials for dyeing

When collecting and experimenting with natural dye-stuffs, remember that different colours can be drawn from the various parts of the plants including leaves, stalk, bark and root, as well as flower. When gathering plants there are no set rules, although most plants are best used fresh even though many dry well and can be used successfully at a later date. If wild flowers are used, always consider carefully the continuance of the species in its habitat. In storing plants, it is important to make certain that plants are thoroughly dried before putting in a container for a later use. As a rule, most plants are best collected young, particularly flowers, which should be used well before they run to seed. Berries and seeds should be used ripe. Most roots are best gathered in autumn although there are exceptions such as meadowsweet, which is at its best in early summer. Bark, if resinous, is generally collected in the spring, otherwise autumn. Lichens, if they must be collected, are easier to gather after a rainy spell.

All parts of the plants are soaked overnight, although walnut hulls and similar dye sources need longer. It is advisable to chop the leaves, twigs, bark, etc. before soaking. Berries, seeds and other fruits should be crushed. Presoaking is just as important for preparation of the numerous powdered and dried natural dyestuffs available from suppliers.

Mordanting

All dyes belong to one of two classes: substantive, those dyes which require no preparation for imparting their colour direct to the fibres, or adjective, those dyes which

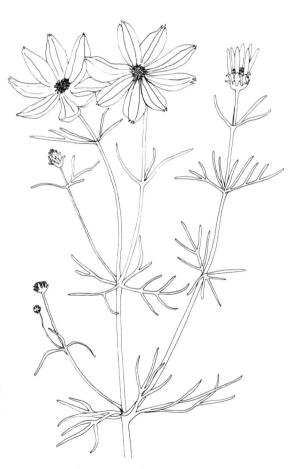

Coreopsis (*Coreopsis* species)

78

require a special preparation called mordanting, which involves the application of certain chemical agents to the fibres for the purpose of fixing the colour. Mordanting is essential in most instances if the dye is to take evenly and remain relatively permanent. Success in dyeing, therefore, depends on the careful selection and application of the metallic salts used as mordants.

There are several ways in which mordants can be used: the fibres can be simmered in them either before or after dyeing or they can be added in small quantities to the dyebath.

In selecting a mordant, the basic guide is that the substance applied should affect the physical characteristics of the fibres as little as possible. There is a wide range of metallic salts used by home dyers, but the most frequently used mordants are the following:

Alum (potassium aluminium sulphate) is a white powder that is easily obtainable and relatively inexpensive. If an excessive amount of alum is used, wool becomes sticky to the touch. Alum is most useful for fixing colours when the wool is mordanted first and then dyed. Cream of tartar is usually used in combination with alum as it brightens the colour. Quantities for mordanting with alum:

    100 grams (3.5 oz) alum
     30 grams (1 oz) cream of tartar
    500 grams (17.5 oz) dried weight of scoured wool
Follow the general methods for mordanting.

Chrome: (potassium dichromate or bichromate) is a powdery orange crystal which is sensitive to light; this sensitivity can cause uneven dyeing and, therefore, the mordanting bath and mordanted wool should be exposed to light as little as possible. Chrome, as a mordant, tends to make wool soft and silky, yet an excessive amount can affect the colour. It can be used either in a mordanting bath, similar to alum, or as an additive during dyeing.
Quantities for mordanting with chrome:
    15 grams (0.5 oz) potassium dichromate
    500 grams (17.5 oz) dried weight of scoured wool
Follow the general methods for mordanting.
To use chrome as an additive: add 5 to 10 grams (0.2 to 0.4 oz) of potassium dichromate to the dyebath.

Tin: (stannous chloride) is a white crystal which is most successful as an additive to the dyebath where it intensifies and brightens the colour. Excessive amounts in the mordant bath makes the fibres hard and brittle. It can be just as effective when used as an additive to the dye-

Golden Rod (*Solidago* species)

79

bath and this method involves less risk of damage to the fibres.

Quantities for mordanting with tin:

15 grams (0.5 oz) stannous chloride
60 grams (2 oz) cream of tartar
500 grams (17.5 oz) dried weight of scoured wool

Follow the general method for mordanting.

To use tin as an additive: add 5 to 10 grams (0.2 to 0.4 oz) of stannous chloride to a dyebath per 500 grams (17.5 oz) of wool. Follow the general methods for using metallic salts as additives.

Iron (ferrous sulphate) known also as copperas or green vitriol, is a pale green crystalline powder which, unless properly used, can harden wool. It can be used as a mordant but again it is safer when used as an additive. Small amounts will darken or sadden colours.

To use iron as an additive: add 5 to 10 grams (0.2 to 0.4 oz) of ferrous sulphate with 30 grams (1 oz) of cream of tartar to the dyebath.

Meadowsweet (*Filipendula ulmaria*)

Other useful agents are:

Ammonia (ammonium hydroxide) is used as an aid in extracting colour from lichens. A few drops of ammonia added to the dyebath will in many instances brighten, or even change, colours. In order to test whether the addition of ammonia to the bath would be useful, fill a small glass jar with water to approximately the temperature of the dyebath. Add a drop or two of ammonia to this and enter a sample of the dyed fibre to the jar, remove, rinse and compare with an untreated sample.

Cream of Tartar (acid potassium tartaric) is a white powder, readily obtainable. It is used with the mordant agents to brighten colours.

Acetic Acid or vinegar is used to neutralize alkaline dye baths and can heighten some colours. It is particularly useful as it is not harmful to vegetable fibres either in solution or on drying.

Tannic acid used in the form of tannin substances has little affinity for wool, and although these substances can make it harsh they are used in wool dyebaths to precipitate impurities which would otherwise spoil the clarity of the dye. They are readily absorbed by the vegetable fibres, however, and form insoluble compounds in the fibre to which the dyestuffs become fixed.

80

Methods for mordanting

The quantities required are indicated under the specific metallic salt above; the general method is as follows: Dissolve the mordant thoroughly in sufficient water to cover the fibres completely; 500 grams (17.5 oz) of dried scoured wool require about 15 litres (4 gallons) so make sure the pot is large enough for the quantity to be mordanted, and that the mordant is dissolved completely otherwise the dyeing may be patchy.

Slowly raise the temperature of the mordant bath until warm; when warm, enter the moist wool that has been previously scoured and rinsed. If dyeing in the skein, make certain the skeins are properly tied (see Chapter 6), but not so tightly as to prevent the mordant and dye from penetrating. With the wool immersed in the pot, gradually raise the temperature to boiling point.

Simmer from $\frac{3}{4}$ to 1 hour below the boiling point; remember to turn the wool occasionally so that the mordant will take evenly, but not so frequently as to cause felting.

Allow the bath to cool until the wool can be handled easily. Remove the wool from the mordant bath and either press or squeeze gently to remove the excess liquid.

If dyeing is to follow soon, it can be stored damp but this is advisable only for a few days. The mordanted wool can be thoroughly dried and stored for later use, but must be dampened before entering the dye-bath.

Method for using metallic salts as additives

Remove the wool being dyed from the bath.

Fill a heatproof glass jar with a quantity of the dye liquid from the bath and dissolve the measured additives as thoroughly as possible in the hot liquid.

Return this liquid to the bath and continue simmering and stirring until the additives are thoroughly dissolved. Return the wool to the bath keeping it completely immersed until the desired shade is obtained. Remember that wet wool is slightly darker than when dry. Follow the rinsing procedure used for dyeing.

Mordanting linen and cotton

Plant fibres require a special mordanting preparation because of the difference in their chemical properties. They do not generally receive natural dye colours as effectively as wool. Considerable time is needed in mordanting cotton and linen.

Quantities needed to mordant:

    60 grams (2 oz) sodium carbonate (washing soda)
    300 grams (10.5 oz) alum
    30 grams (1 oz) tannic acid
    500 grams (17.5 oz) dried scoured fibres

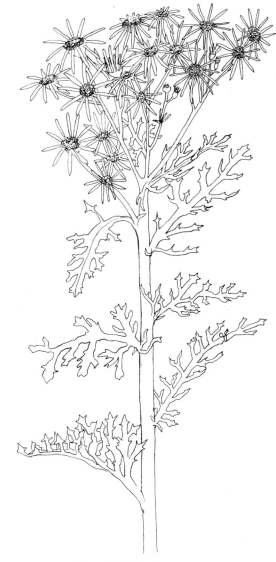

Ragwort (*Senecio jacobaea*)

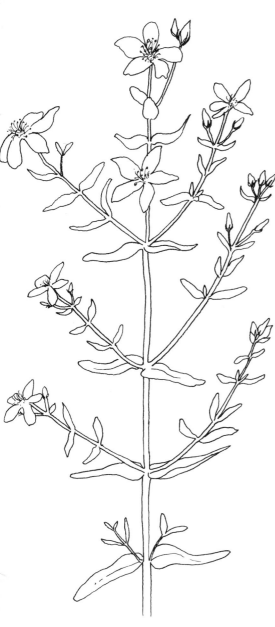

Dissolve 30 grams (1 oz) sodium carbonate and 150 grams (5.2 oz) alum in 15 litres (4 gallons) of clear soft water.

Enter the moistened skeins in the mordant bath and slowly raise the temperature to boiling and maintain for one hour. Leave to stand overnight in the cooling liquid.

The next day, prepare the 30 grams (1 oz) tannic acid with the same quantity of water, 15 litres (4 gallons), and enter the well rinsed skeins into this bath.

Raise the temperature gradually to 60–70°C (140–160°F) and maintain for one hour while moving the fibres in the bath. Again leave it to stand overnight in the cooling bath.

The third day, prepare the remaining half of sodium carbonate and alum in the same quantity of clear water. Enter the rinsed skeins and, as before, gradually raise the temperature and boil for one hour. Leave overnight and rinse, prior to dyeing on the fourth day.

Mordanting silk

Spun silk must be thoroughly degummed (see chapter 4) prior to mordanting and dyeing, but other than that, the fibre can be dealt with in the same manner as wool although the temperature of either mordant or dyebath should not exceed 70°C (160°F). Silk generally requires double the ingredients of dyestuffs. Because it easily mats, it is advisable to lift the skeins in and out of the bath, rather than turning them over with a stick.

Methods for dyeing wool

Prepare the dyebath the night before by chopping or crushing the plant material and filling the pot with sufficient water just to cover the dyestuffs and later, wool. Many dyers find it practical to put the chopped materials into a muslin or cheesecloth bag which can easily be removed when the bath is ready for the wool; the use of such a bag is practical if equipment for straining large quantities is not available.

The following day, slowly raise the temperature of the dyebath until just below the boiling point; the length of time depending on the colour extracted. If using a powdered natural dye, make certain it is thoroughly dissolved before altering the temperature.

In order to separate the plant material from the fibres, either strain the liquid into a different pot or remove the containing bag; this is particularly advisable if dyeing skeins where an even colour is required. Or, provided there is room in the pot, enter the wool into the dye-

Saint John's Wort (*Hypericum* species)

bath along with the dye material. This technique is entirely satisfactory when dyeing in the fleece as any unevenness of colour can be removed by blending during carding, and more intense colours are usually obtained. After the dyebath is cooled, moisten and then enter the scoured wool, whether mordanted or not, into the dyebath. Keep the bath on the simmer as boiling can destroy colours. Check the colouring action on the fibre by periodically removing samples.

It is necessary to make certain that the dye penetrates all parts of the fibre; do this by occasionally turning it over, although excessive stirring should be avoided to prevent the wool from matting.

As long as there is colour in the dyebath it can be used, although subsequent batches of wool will be lighter. If the amount of liquid in the bath gets low, remove the wool, add boiling water, stir and return the wool to the bath. When the desired shade is achieved, remove the wool and rinse in hot, clear water until colour no longer runs out. Squeeze or press excess water from the wool and leave it to dry away from the sun in a manner similar to that used after scouring.

When using natural dyes, make certain that a sufficient quantity of wool is dyed, as it is difficult to reproduce colours exactly in subsequent baths. Some dye liquids can be stored for later use, but this is not always successful. Always test stored liquid dyes before use to avoid disappointment or disaster.

Dyeing in the skein usually produces a more intense colour than dyeing in the fleece, although the latter allows for more numerous colour possibilities by blending, so this is often a more rewarding technique for handspinners. The other consideration is that by taking advantage of the fresh plant materials and newly shorn fleeces, a spinner can spend the warmer days colouring his fibres for later winter spinning.

Basic recipe

The standard recipe for natural dyes is:
    equal weights of plant material and wool
    sufficient water to just cover dyestuffs and wool
Variations do exist; for instance many of the ground, powdered natural dyestuffs go further while the quantity of some fresh plants needs to be increased.

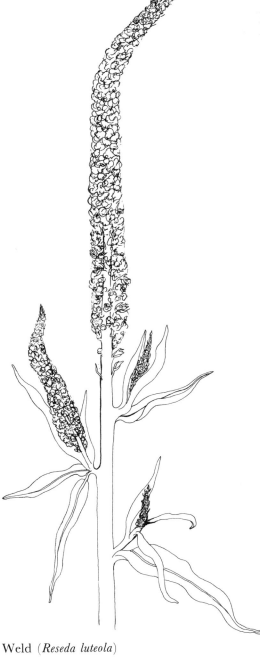

Weld (*Reseda luteola*)

Alkanet (*Alkanna* or *Anchusa tinctoria*)

Bedstraw (*Galium verum*)

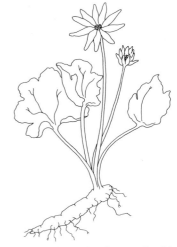

Bloodroot (*Sanguinaria canadensis*)

Guide to dyestuffs

Dye substance	Ratio dye: wool	Part used	Source	Mordant and colour
Agrimony *Agrimonia eupatoria*	4:1	leaves and stalks	Collect fresh	Alum – yellow Chrome – yellow
Alkanet *Alkanna* or *Anchusa tinctoria*	½:1	roots	Collect fresh/ available commercially	No mordant – grey-blue Alum – reddish brown
Apple *Pyrus malus*	1:1	bark	Collect fresh	Alum – yellow (fresh) tan (dried) Iron – green
Annatto *Bixa orellana*	½:1	seeds	Available commercially powdered	Alum – orange
Bedstraw *Galium verum*	4:1 1:1	tops roots	Collect fresh	Alum/Chrome – yellow Alum/Chrome – reds
Birch *Betula* species	2:1	leaves	Collect fresh	Alum – yellow
Blackberry *Rubus* species	1:1	vines	Collect fresh in spring	Alum with Iron – grey
Bloodroot *Sanguinaria canadensis*	1:1	roots	Collect fresh/available commercially	Alum – oranges
Bracken *Pteris aquilinum*	4:1	fronds/young shoots	Collect in spring	Alum – yellowish green
Broom *Cytisus scoparius*	2:1	flowering ·branches	Collect fresh	Alum/Chrome – yellow

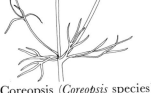

Coreopsis (*Coreopsis* species)　　　　Fustic (*Chlorophora tinctoria*)

Dye substance	Ratio dye : wool	Part used	Source	Mordant and colour
Cochineal *Coccus cacti*	$\frac{1}{4}$: 1	whole insect	Available commercially whole/ powdered	Alum – pinkish red Chrome – purple Oxalic acid and Tin – brighter red
Coreopsis *Coreopsis tinctoria*	1 : 1	flowers	Collect fresh	No mordant – yellow Alum – gold Tin – rusty orange Chrome – rust Iron – green
Cutch *Acacia catechu* or *Areca catechu*	$\frac{1}{2}$: 1	wood, nuts or seed pods	Available commercially powdered	No mordant – tan Alum – brown
Dahlia *Dahlia* species	2 : 1	flower	Collect fresh	Alum/Chrome – yellow
Dock *Rumex obtusifolius*	$\frac{1}{2}$: 1	roots	Collect fresh	Alum – yellows
Dog's mercury *Mercurialis perennis*	2 : 1	whole	Collect fresh	Alum – yellow
Dyer's greenwood *Genista tinctoria*	2 : 1	flowering branches	Collect fresh	Alum/Chrome – yellows
Elder *Sambucus nigra*	2 : 1 2 : 1	leaves berries	Collect fresh	Alum – greeny yellow Alum/Acetic acid – violet
Fustic *Chlorophora tinctoria*	1 : 1	bark	Available commercially	Alum/Chrome – yellows

Logwood (*Haematoxylon campechia-num*)

Madder (*Rubia tinctorum*)

Golden Rod (*Solidago* species)

Marigold (*Tagetes* species)

Dye substance	Ratio dye: wool	Part used	Source	Mordant and colour
Golden marguerite *Anthemis tinctoria*	2:1	flowers	Collect fresh	Alum/Chrome – yellows/golds
Golden rod *Solidago* species	2:1	flowers	Collect fresh	Alum – yellowy greens Chrome – bronze Iron – green Tin – yellowy orange
Henna *Lawsonia inermis*	$\frac{1}{2}$:1	leaves	Available commercially	Tin – reddish brown
Indigo *Indigofera tinctoria*		leaves	Available commercially powdered	Blue. Not soluble in water – requires special preparation
Juniper *Juniperus communis*	1:1	berries	Collect/available commercially	Alum – tannish yellow
Lily of the valley *Convallaria majalis*	2:1	leaves	Collect fresh	Alum – greenish yellow (spring) Chrome – bronze
Logwood *Haematoxylon campechianum*	$\frac{1}{4}$:1	bark	Available commercially as chips	No mordant – blue Alum – dark purple Chrome – dark blue
Madder *Rubia tinctorum*	$\frac{1}{2}$:1 1:1	roots – powdered roots – chopped	Available commercially	Alum – red Chrome – rust
Marigold *Tagetes* species	2:1	flowers	Collect fresh/available commercially	Alum – greenish gold Tin – orangey gold

Meadowsweet
(*Filipendula ulmaria*)

Ragwort (*Senecio jacobaea*)

Saint John's Wort
(*Hypericum* species)

Dye substance	Ratio dye: wool	Part used	Source	Mordant and colour
Meadowsweet *Filipendula ulmaria*	4:1	whole plant	Collect fresh	Alum – greeny yellow
Mullein *Verbascum thapsus*	4:1	stalks, leaves	Collect fresh	Alum/Chrome – yellow
Nettle *Urtica dioica*	4:1	stalks, leaves	Collect fresh	Alum/Chrome – greenish yellow
Onion *Allium cepa*	1:1 3:1	skins whole	Collect fresh	Alum – golden tan Chrome – bronze Tin – orange Iron – green
Privet *Ligustrum vulgare*	2:1	leaves	Collect fresh	Alum – yellow Iron – green Chrome – brass
Queen Anne's lace (wild carrot) *Daucus carota*	4:1	flowers, stems, leaves	Collect fresh	Alum – yellow
Ragwort *Senecio jacobaea*	2:1	flowering tops	Collect fresh	Alum – yellow Iron – green
Safflower *Carthamus tinctorius*	4:1	flowers	Collect fresh/available commercially	Alum – yellow
Saffron *Crocus sativus*	$\frac{1}{4}$:1	stigmas	Collect fresh/ available commercially	Alum – golden yellow
Saint John's wort *Hypericum* species	3:1	flowering tops	Collect fresh	Alum – yellowy green

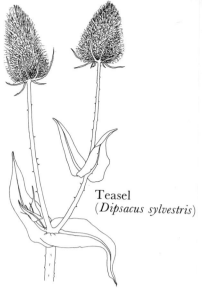

Teasel
(*Dipsacus sylvestris*)

Tansey (*Tanacetum vulgare*)

Sumac (*Rhus* species)

Dye substance	Ratio dye : wool	Part used	Source	Mordant and colour
Sanderswood *Pterocarpus santalinus*	1 : 1	bark	Available commercially	Chrome – rusty red
Sumac *Rhus* species	4 : 1 ½ : 1	leaves, shoots berries	Collect fresh	No mordant – tan Alum – yellow tan Iron – grey
Tansey *Tanacetum vulgare*	2 : 1	flowering heads	Collect fresh	Alum – yellow
Teasel *Dipsacus sylvestris*	1 : 1	leaves, flowers	Collect fresh	Alum – yellow
Tomato *Lycopersicon esculentum*	2 : 1	leaves, vines	Collect fresh	Alum with Iron – mint green
Turmeric *Curcuma longa*	½ : 1	root	Available commercially	Alum – yellow Chrome – gold
Walnut *Juglans nigra*	1 : 1	hulls	Collect and dry/ available commercially	No mordant – tan Iron – brown
Weld *Reseda luteola*	2 : 1	whole plant	Collect fresh/or dried	Alum/Chrome – yellow Iron – green
Woad *Isatis tinctoria*		leaves	Collect fresh	Blue. Requires a special fermentation process

Fastness of dyes

Although fastness is a great concern particularly when the fibres will be employed in an article intended for use, the dyer must realize that no dye is absolutely fast under all conditions. A dye may be fast on one fibre and not on another, or fast to light but not washing. To check for fastness to light the simplest method, although not conclusive, is to expose a sample of the dyed fibre to direct sunlight for a few days. This sample is later compared to another from the same lot which has not been subjected to the same light exposure.

To determine whether a dye will fade in washing, a sample must be given several washings under the washing conditions it will be subjected to, and then the dried sample should be compared to the original unwashed sample. Remember that felting will alter the colour.

A dyer should keep labelled samples and recipes for all dyebaths attempted as a record, so that successes can be duplicated and failures never repeated. Samples should be mounted in a binder and referenced with information on quantity, variations of methods, results of mordants or additives, and fastness which can be recorded on index cards that can be tacked near the stove while dyeing.

Weld (*Reseda luteola*)

Variations through dyeing

Top-dyeing, which involves dipping the fibres into two or more dyebaths of different colour in order to obtain a third hue, extends the colour range. For example, wool mordanted with alum can be dyed in an onion dyebath to produce yellow, rinsed and then dipped into an indigo dyebath; the result is a striking olive green. The opposite ordering of the dyebaths, indigo followed by onion, produces a more blue-green colour.

Another variation is tie-dyeing, which involves the selective or random tying of a skein so that the dye is unable to penetrate, or top-dyeing sections of the skein to produce a second colour. If the dye is to be kept from penetrating a section of the skein, it must be tightly and securely wrapped with cotton thread.

In addition, dyeing offers the spinner several variations which he may wish to explore during yarn design. Dyed wool can be blended during fibre preparation or spinning, or two or more colours can be plied together, as discussed in the next chapter.

Woad (*Isatis tinctoria*)

6 Yarn design

There is a tendency even among handspinners themselves to conceive of handspun yarn as imperfect, rough and irregular, almost crude in appearance. This is a regrettable concept and one that should be examined in both its positive and negative aspects. Handspinning is no longer a necessity, although the product has a utilitarian function, but possesses the additional advantage that there is scope for contemporary handspinning to be forward-looking in design. The handspinner today is in a situation where he can give creative thought and the additional time to designing a yarn which is more than simply functional.

Designing involves two areas: fibre preparation and spinning. The final outcome should not be accidental, but rather the result of controlled preparation and spinning. In other words, all the processes that are involved in preparing the fibres prior to the actual process of spinning, as well as the spinning and finishing of yarn, are an essential part of yarn design and none of the steps should be neglected, but rather creatively explored and employed.

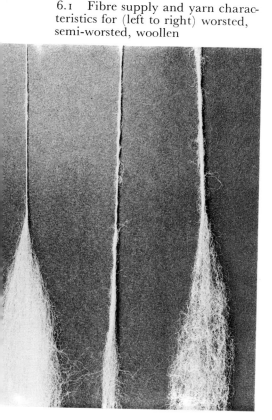

6.1 Fibre supply and yarn characteristics for (left to right) worsted, semi-worsted, woollen

Design within fibre preparation

The initial way the fibres are prepared and arranged prior to spinning will determine the yarn's textural characteristics.

Worsted, semi-worsted, woollen

The method used for arranging the fibres has a significant influence on the yarn produced. A worsted yarn characteristically has a smooth surface as it is spun from long staple fibres that have previously been prepared in a parallel arrangement by combing. Where the arrangement has included both long and short fibres that have been drawn into parallel arrangements through teasing, the spun yarn has a more hairy appearance than a true worsted and is called semi-worsted, because although the majority of the fibres lie parallel and along the yarn there are some that lie across the yarn and break up the smooth appearance with protruding stray fibres. A semi-worsted yarn lies between a worsted and a woollen.

In woollen yarns fibres of irregular length are arranged by carding and spun with the fibres lying at right angles to the completed yarn. This arrangement traps more air than a worsted yarn resulting in a yarn that is both hairy and spongey. The technique for preparing fibres in these arrangements can be found in Chapter 2.

Commercially prepared fibres

Handspinners are more and more coming in contact with an increasing number of commercially prepared fibres which are arranged for the commercial yarn manufacturer. In the early days of the Industrial Revolution, handspinners took full advantage of these prepared fibres if their economic situation permitted. In America, fleeces were taken to the local carding mill where the fibres were prepared and taken home for spinning. In Yorkshire, the combing craft developed to supply the cottage spinner and later the manufacturer until it too was replaced by machinery.

There are basically two industrial methods of preparing the fibres, combing and carding. A combed arrangement is usually termed a top and has a very smooth uniform appearance with all the fibres lying parallel to its length. When spinning from a top, it is advantageous to split it down its length one or more times to aid drafting. It is best spun by using a short-draw method with an extended drafting region (fig. 6.2). By employing a twisting movement with the drafting hand, the fibre supply is given a bit more pull which aids drafting and also takes the fibres uniformly throughout the top. The yarn spun from a worsted top is designed to be smooth and consistent. The parallel fibres, however, require more twist than carded fibres. If the spinner does not want to retain the regularity of the combed top, the fibres can be fluffed and the top opened by shaking before spinning.

In commercially carded wool, referred to as a sliver, the direction of the fibres is unlike that obtained by handcarding as the fibres have not been rolled. Some of the fibres tend to lie in a random orientation although the majority lie parallel to the direction of the spun fibre. Their length is not consistent and they are also much shorter and more irregular than those found in combed tops. Again it is often advantageous to split the rovings prior to spinning. The spinning technique is usually determined by the consistency of the roving.

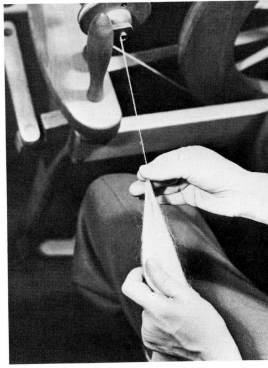

6.2 An extended draw is used when spinning worsted

91

6.3　Yarns designed during fibre preparation (top to bottom):
Contrasting colours and texture blended.
Fibres blended on carders, cashmere and wool.
Noils introduced on carders prior to forming the rolag.
Garnetted wool introduced during carding.

Blending

Fibre blending provides an effective means of achieving further variation in the texture of the yarn. It can take several forms. The most common is blending different matchings from a fleece which may be useful for several reasons. Occasionally, a spinner discovers when sorting fibres that there is not a sufficient quantity of matching fibres either of crimp, staple, length or texture to produce the desired amount of yarn. In order to prevent irregularities in the quality of the spun fibres which could cause difficulties, such as irregular shrinkage, felting or uncontrolled texture variation it is necessary to blend the different matchings from the beginning. It is also a means of using the different qualities of wool composing a fleece, for often neck, leg, even belly wool is clean, but not suitable, or in quantity for use on its own. As long as it is not damaged, it can be blended and a large waste of raw materials eliminated. Blending for the purpose of mixing fibre characteristics is most difficult as consistency is critical if the response of the yarn when finished is to be uniform. First tease the separate qualities to be used and give an initial carding to further open and arrange the fibres. Then remove them from the card as a flat carded layer. Mix these layers in proportion by spreading layers of different matchings in turn across the carder, then carding and preparing the rolag in the usual manner.

The same technique employed in blending different matchings is used to mix different fibres. Sometimes this form of blending is used to give strength, to control short fibres such as dog's hair, or to produce a textured design in the yarn. The textural characteristics of the fibres are accentuated when the blending involves mixing long and short staple fibres. The proportion of the fibres used in the blend is dependent on the textural characteristic which is to be emphasized. The blending of different fibres can be achieved in the same manner as the blending of different matchings or one of the fibres can be introduced during the carding of the other by layering it across the carder and letting the carding process randomly mix the two. To produce a semi-worsted yarn, the carded fibres can be removed as a layer rather than rolled to form a rolag and drawn by hand into a parallel arrangement (see Chapter 2).

Another blending variation is the use of colour, either natural or dyed. It can be approached in the same manner as the blending of different matchings so that a third or new colour is created or the proportions can be varied and the consistency of the blend to produce a randomly mixed effect. A wide range of variations can be achieved by mixing proportions and colour on the carders.

A technique for providing texture is by the introduction of noils which create a nub effect in the spun yarn. Noils are the waste bits, such as second cuts, that the handspinner attempts to eliminate during fibre preparation. By rolling short fibre bits between the fingers to create tiny balls, a sufficient quantity can be made to supplement those collected from previous preparation. Introduce the noils either by sprinkling the carder with them prior to forming the rolag or by inserting them at regular intervals while spinning. An alternative to the use of noils is the introduction of garnett, short lengths of spun yarn. Pick over and open these short lengths either by hand or coarse carding and, as with the noils, scatter them across the carders prior to the formation of a rolag. Variation in colour and texture is produced by introducing noils or garnetted yarn of contrasting colour to the predominate colour of the fibre supply.

Design within spinning

The design potential of handspun yarn is further extended by the process of spinning. This, however, requires considerable skill on the part of the spinner who must be able to control textural variations in a consistent manner.

Slub formation, which plagues the handspinner in the learning process, can be induced purposely for a textured design effect. Slubs are the short, heavy irregularities in the yarn which are the result of intermittent drafting. By using a short-draw technique, the spinner drafts more fibres than required for the count of the yarn; the pressure from the fingers guiding the twist up the fibre arrangement is then released and 'skips' over the extra fibres creating a slub.

Unspun fibres can be added on to the yarn as it is produced. This involves holding a quantity of carded fibres against the twisting zone of the yarn so that a small amount is caught up as it is spun. A variation is the use of two rolags, unlike in colour or texture, that are blended during drafting to produce completely different results.

The most basic design variations in spinning are the degrees and types of twist. The texture of the yarn is influenced by the former. The correct twist is that which holds the fibres together with sufficient strength for its finished purpose. By imposing only a light (low) twist on the prepared fibres, the result is a soft yarn which sacrifices strength. A yarn of this character can be strengthened by plying with a firmer twisted yarn. The other extreme is the introduction of more twist, either to the degree of strengthening the fibres for their end use or for imposing overtwist as a characteristic of the yarn.

6.4 Yarns designed during spinning (top to bottom):
Introducing slub formation.
Introducing noils.
Blending two rolags of different colours and textures during drafting.
Introducing unspun fibres on the spun yarn while spinning.
Overtwist being allowed to accumulate.
Low Twist.
High Twist.

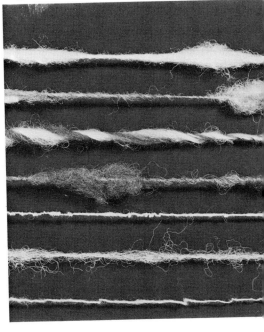

93

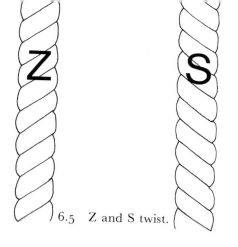

6.5   Z and S twist.

6.6   Yarns designed by plying
(top to bottom):
Two Z twisted singles plied S.
Three ply.
Two Z twisted singles cabled Z.
Z twisted woollen single with an
S twisted linen plied Z.
Two Z twisted singles, one fine
and the other heavy, plied S.
Two Z twisted singles, one slub
and the other fine, plied S.
Spiral yarn created by retarding
one Z twisted while hurrying the
other Z twisted single during S
plying.
Overplied yarn created by retarding
one single while transversing back
and forth with the other to build
up texture.
Overplied yarn with a heavier
build-up of texture.
Introduction of tufts of unspun
during plying.

Remember that worsted and fine yarns require more twist than woollen or bulky yarns. Warp yarns require more strength and therefore more twist than yarns used for weft. If the finished article is to have a smooth firm surface the fibres will require more twist than a soft-textured surface. In planning the amount of twist, remember that plying in the opposite direction to the yarn's initial twist, and also scouring, will reduce the amount of twist before the yarn is ready to be used. It is advisable to add slightly more twist than required in the finished yarn.

Fibres can be spun with either Z or S twist (fig. 6.5). Z twist involves either the handspindle or the wheel being rotated in a clockwise direction. This is the type of twist generally imposed on single-ply animal fibres. When the fibres are twisted in an anti-clockwise direction, the twist is termed S.

Plying and cabling are the most obvious means of creating variety in yarn design through the use of S or Z twists in combinations. Plying means to fold or double; it is a technique of twisting two or more strands of yarns together in the direction opposite to the single twist, whereas cabling is twisting the singles in the same direction as their initial twist.

Experimenting with the technique of plying can produce creative texture and colour effects. The simplest form of plying involves little more than spinning together two twisted singles to produce a two-ply yarn. Single spun yarns are generally plied together with a reverse twist, resulting in a plied yarn which is softer than the original singles of the combination. If two singles are twisted in the same direction as their initial twist then the result is a yarn with a very hard character.

Plying and cabling are an extension of spinning and can be done on the handspindle, great or treadle wheel. The singles to be plied are best managed if they are stored on bobbins or even old yarn cones. Mount either bobbins or cones on a rack so that they run freely and come from the same direction. The same basic principles apply as with the spinning of a single: there is the same drafting area and twisting zone, but the fibre supply takes the form of the two or more singles to be plied. Whatever spinning device is used for doubling, a starting length of the same twist as the twist to be imposed during doubling is required.

Plying on a spindle
Tie a starting length to the spindle in the usual manner and then tie the free end to the ends of the yarns to be doubled. The middle finger of the fibre supply/drafting hand serves as a guide while the yarns pass to the side of it. Draft out the yarns and insert the twist by using

94

the right hand to start the spindle rotating in an anti-clockwise direction for an S twist or clockwise if a Z twist is required. When a sufficient length of the plied yarn has the desired amount of twist, wind on the spindle in the correct direction.

Plying on a treadle wheel

Place the bobbin rack to the left of the spinner with the yarns to be doubled in a direct line with the orifice. Tie the yarns to a starting length and then roll a small quantity across the guide hooks and on to the bobbin before plying begins. The short-draw technique is used but with an increased drafting zone. The left hand drafts and tensions the fibre supply by passing the middle finger through the yarns to be doubled while the twist is guided up the yarn by the lightly pinched thumb and index finger of the right hand (fig. 6.7).

As with the short-draw the operation is consistent with the yarns being drafted, twisted and wound on at the same time. However, the feet now treadle faster while the hands hold the yarn long enough for the desired twist to be imposed. It is important to watch the bobbin and fill it correctly.

Often the purpose of plying is to increase the thickness of the yarn and the orifice of the wheel may not be large enough for such a thickness to pass through. The wheel can be adapted by plugging the orifice with a length of dowel which has had the outer end slightly tapered and sanded (fig. 6.8). Plying is then approached in the same manner as on the great wheel but with the assistance of the treadle.

Plying on the great wheel

Plying on the great wheel requires one alteration, that is, the single belt must be crossed (fig. 6.9) if the twist is to be S. With this crossing of the belt, the wheel can still be turned in a clockwise direction. S twist can obviously be obtained by turning the wheel in an anti-clockwise direction, but this is not as convenient for the spinner because when walking backwards the spokes must be turned below the wheel's axle and an uncomfortable stoop is developed. Tensioning and drafting is done by the left hand with the middle finger passing between the singles. Wind on in the same manner as when spinning a single with the exception that the plied yarn winds on over the top of the spindle.

Besides combining different fibres or colours when plying, variety can also be achieved by using singles of different textures. Further variation can be produced by changing the tension of the singles. The textural combinations are endless and well worth exploring by the handspinner.

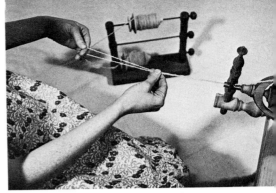

6.7   Plying on a treadle wheel.

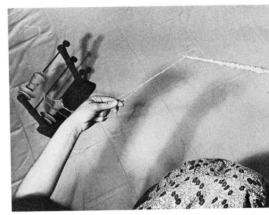

6.8   Plying off a tapered dowel in orifice.

6.9   Belt crossed for plying on the great wheel.

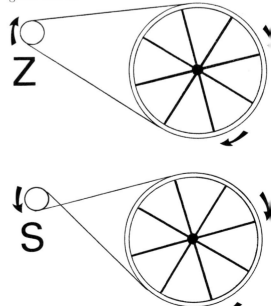

Preparing handspun for use

Skeining

After the fibres have been spun and plied, the final step is to prepare the yarn so it is suitable for use. The yarn must first be removed from the spindle or bobbin and made into skeins for scouring. If the handspindle or spindle of the great wheel has been properly filled, the cop will be loose enough to be slipped off the tapered end and mounted on a bobbin rack and skeined in the same manner as yarn from a bobbin. If skeining directly from the bobbin of the treadle wheel, free the tension of the belt by slipping it off the bobbin pulley. A skein can be made by using the thumbs of both hands as demonstrated (fig. 6.10) although it is difficult to maintain an evenly tensioned or sized skein. A niddy-noddy or stick reel provides a readily portable skein winder with a set diameter. Tie the end of the yarn to be skeined to one end of a cross arm and follow the course illustrated (fig. 6.11). When the bobbin is completely unwound, untie the end originally fastened to the niddy-noddy and join the two ends together (fig. 6.12). Secure the skein in two or three additional places, but not so tightly that the fibres cannot be properly scoured or penetrated by dyes. Grip the skein at both ends, stretch it to its full length and firmly twist in the direction of the yarn's twist. Then fold in half, which will further twist the skein (fig. 6.13), and secure the two ends of the hank in one another before storing. The same method of securing the skeins should be used if a click reel is employed.

Scouring

The next stage is the scouring of the yarn; this can be most critical to the final finish obtained in the handspun. Fibres which felt easily, and this includes wool and wool combinations, should be steeped in hand-hot soft water and left until the water cools before scouring. Even when the yarn has been steeped, the scouring process requires care.

Fill a tub with sudsy water, immerse the skeins and allow them to soak freely. Handle as little as possible and leave overnight if convenient. Rinse in a clear bath of warm water and gently squeeze or press out the excess water. On no account should the skeins be subjected to running water. If a second or third bath is required to free the oils, prepare these in the same manner as the first but with the temperature of each slightly reduced. Remember that extremes of water temperature, excessive handling and wringing all cause felting.

All fibres vary in the amount of scouring they require. Spun silk will require boiling to remove the gum. Linen can be softened prior to bleaching by boiling for about

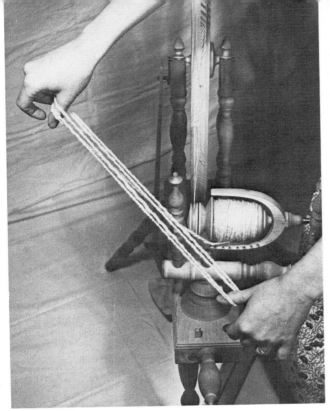

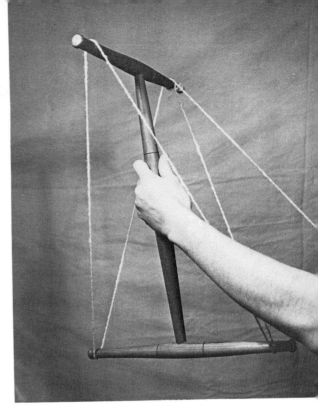

6.10 Skeining with thumbs. Belt removed from bobbin pulley so that the bobbin runs freely.

6.11 Skeining with a niddy-noddy.

6.12 Tying the skein

6.13 Folding the skein

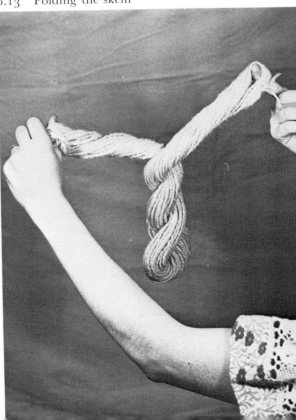

an hour or so in soapy water and then rubbing the yarn as the water cools. Cotton may respond to a light scouring, but if particularly soiled it too can be boiled in soapy water.

Dry the skeins either with or without tension. Drying under tension does help to remove some overtwist but reduces the elasticity of the yarn and gives it a permanent set. Skeins can be tensioned by hanging a suitable sized weight in the skein as it dries. If tensioning is not required, simply suspend the skeins from a dowel or drying rack without the addition of weights. While the yarn is still slightly damp it can be wound off onto a reel and the yarn set in this manner. If the skeins are to be forced dried, the temperature must be low. Dry them properly and check the ties prior to storage.

Guide to yarn count

System	Name	Unit of length	Unit of weight
Woollen (Galashiels)	cut	200 yards	1 lb
Woollen (Cut USA)	cut	300 yards	1 lb
Worsted (Continental)	hank	1000 metres	1 kg
Worsted (English)	skein	560 yards	1 lb
Linen (Irish)	lea	300 yards	1 lb
Spun silk	denier	840 yards	1 lb
Cotton (Continental)	hank	2000 metres	1 kg
Cotton (English)	hank	840 yards	1 lb

The count system has been developed over the centuries to describe the different sizes of yarn. Because of its antiquity, no uniform system was developed for all fibres and methods of spinning, but usually the count number was taken as the number of skeins of some standard length of yarn contained in a standard weight. To further confuse the matter, the name given to the standard length and its size was also variable (hanks, leas, skeins, cuts).

In the continental worsted system, for example, the count is the number of hanks of 1000 m length contained in 1 kilogram of yarn. A yarn for which 20 of these hanks weighed 1 kilogram would be written 20s. When yarns are plied the count given is for the individual constituent yarns and a number prefix is used to designate the number of such yarns twisted together: 2/20s, 3/20s, 4/20s represents 2, 3 and 4 20s-count yarns plied together. In silk yarns the ordering is reversed: 20/2, 20/3, etc.

This system is now being replaced by the TEX system which has been reached by international agreement and is the same for all fibres. In this system, the count of the yarn is the weight in grams of one kilometre of yarn.

To find the count of homespun, weigh a skein of known length in a consistent set of units, metric or imperial.

Tex system

$$\text{Count} = \frac{\text{weight (grams)}}{\text{length (metres)}} \times 1000$$

Other metric systems

$$\text{Count} = \frac{\text{standard weight (grams)}}{\text{weight of skein (grams)}} \times \frac{\text{number of metres in hank}}{\text{number of metres in standard}}$$

Other imperial systems

$$\text{Count} = \frac{\text{standard weight (ounces)}}{\text{weight of skein (ounces)}} \times \frac{\text{number of yards in hank}}{\text{number of yards in standard}}$$

Uses of handspun

The end result of spinning is the incorporation of the yarn into a finished article, and therefore it is necessary from the moment the article is conceived to produce a yarn having suitable characteristics for the use for which it is intended. This comes from experience as the range of crafts that handspun yarn can be employed in is quite considerable and the yarns needed for weaving, crochet, embroidery, knitting, needlework, lacemaking or macramé can differ considerably. Some indication of the qualities needed can be obtained by studying the characteristics of machine-spun yarns marketed for the craft one wishes to explore. Note the characteristics that should be incorporated into a yarn, then make samples and test them for the qualities desired in the finished article before starting on a large project. Create a yarn with a purpose, but do not hesitate to experiment and explore the unknown!

99

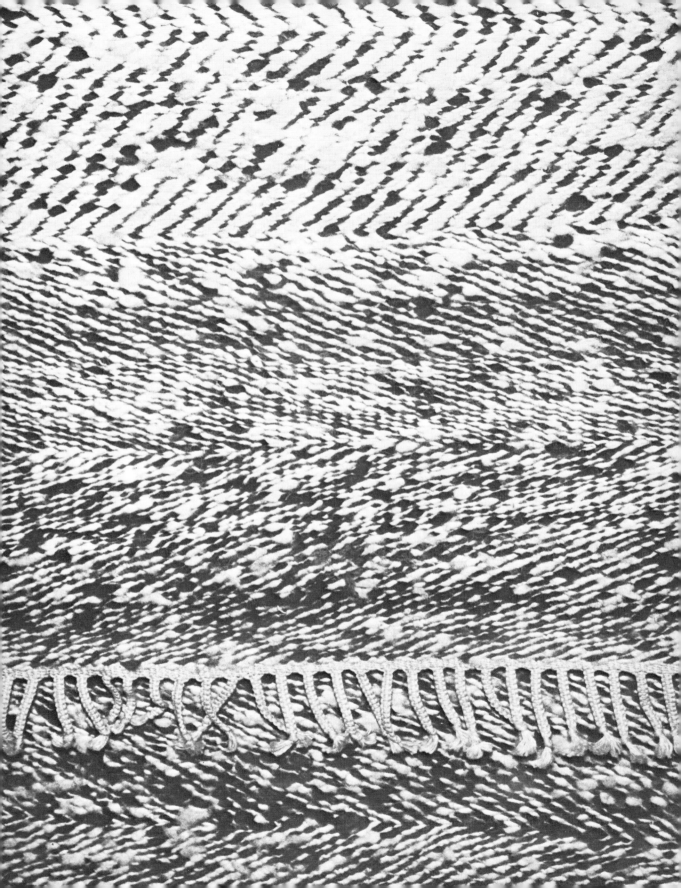

Flat rug woven with handspun
natural-coloured woollen weft by
Tony Reed

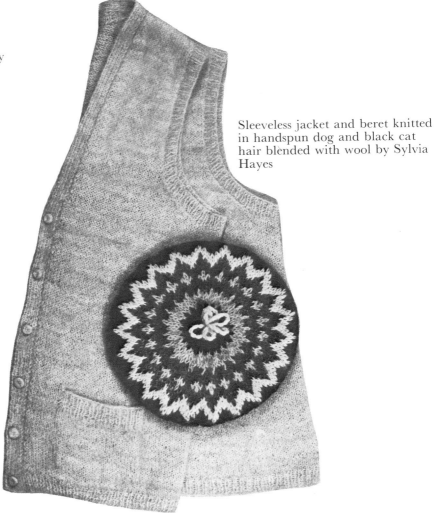

Sleeveless jacket and beret knitted
in handspun dog and black cat
hair blended with wool by Sylvia
Hayes

Puritan collar woven and trimmed
with bobbin lace from unbleached
linen by Rita Acton

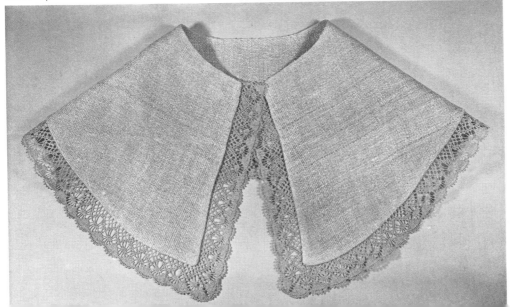

Sherpa's jacket woven in handspun
wool and alpaca by Sylvia Hayes

Textured tapestry in handspun
wool by Sylvia Hayes

Suppliers

United Kingdom

British Wool Marketing Board   Educational materials
Kew Bridge House,   Fleeces
Kew Bridge Road
Isleworth, Middlesex

Craftsman's Mark Ltd   Wool matchings
Trefnant   Rovings
Denbigh LL165UD, North Wales

K. R. Drummond   Books
30 Hart Grove
Ealing Common, London

Handweaver's Studio   Spinning wheels and equipment
29 Haroldstone Road   Fibres and dyes
London E17 7AN   Tuition

Frank Herring and Sons   Spinning wheels and equipment
27 High West Street
Dorchester, Dorset

Eliza Leadbeater   Spinning wheels and equipment
Rookery Cottage,   Natural and chemical dyes, mordants
Dalefords Lane   and equipment
Whitegate   Fibres, fleeces, books and repairs
Northwich, Cheshire   Workshops and tuition

Matheson Dyes and Chemicals   Natural and chemical dyes
Marcon Place   Mordants
London E8 1LP

Uni-Dye   Chemical dyes
P.O. Box No. 10
Ilkley, Yorkshire

North America

Albion Hills Farm and School
of Spinning and Weaving
R. R. No 3
Caledon East, Ontario

Spinning wheels and equipment
Fibres, fleeces and repairs
Tuition and workshops

Black Sheep Weaving and Craft
Supply
318 S W 2nd Street
Corvallis, Oregon 97330

North America only
Books, spinning wheels and equipment
Natural and chemical dyes and
  mordants

Clemes and Clemes
665 San Pablo Avenue
Pinole, California 94564

Spinning equipment

Colonial Textiles
82 Plants Dam Road
East Lyme, Conn. 06333

Spinning wheels and equipment
Natural and chemical dyes and
  mordants
Fibres, fleeces, books and repairs
Tuition and workshops

Earth Guild Inc.
149 Putnam Avenue
Cambridge, Mass. 02139

Spinning equipment
Natural and chemical dyes

Gordon's Naturals
P.O. Box 506
Roseburg, Oregon 97470

Spinning wheels and equipment
Natural dyes and mordants
Fibres and books

Greentree Ranch Wools
163 N. Carter Lake Road
Loveland, Colorado 80537

Spinning equipment
Fibres and books

Handcraft Wools
Box 378
Streetsville, Ontario

Spinning equipment
Chemical dyes
Fibres and books

Mannings Creative Crafts
R.D. 2, East Berlin
Pennsylvania 17316

Spinning equipment
Natural and chemical dyes and
  mordants
Books, fibres and workshops

Northwest Handcraft House Ltd
110 West Esplanade
North Vancouver,
British Columbia

Spinning equipment
Natural and chemical dyes and
  mordants
Books and fibres

Some Place
2990 Adeline Street
Berkeley, California 94703

Spinning equipment
Chemical dyes
Books

Spincraft
P.O. Box 332
Richardson, Texas 75080

US sales only
Spinning equipment

The Spinster 34 Hamilton Avenue Sloatsburg, New York 10974	Spinning equipment Natural dyes and mordants Fibres
Straw into Gold P.O. Box 2904 Oakland, California 94618	Spinning wheels and equipment Natural and chemical dyes and mordants Fleeces, fibres, books and seeds
Tapestry Bay Street Village Bellingham, Washington 98225	Fleeces and books
Traditional Handcrafts 571 Randolph Street Northville, Michigan 48167	Spinning equipment Natural dyes Books
Unicorn Craft and Hobby Book Service Box 645 D Rockville, Md. 20851	Books
Wide World of Herbs Ltd 11 St Catherine Street East Montreal, Canada	Natural dyes and mordants

Other

D. Bailey 15 Dutton Street Bankstown N.S.W. 2200, Australia	Natural dyes
Cambridge Wools Ltd P.O. Box 2572 Auckland, New Zealand	Spinning wheels and equipment Fleece and carded wool
The Homespun Centre 245 Parnell Road Auckland, New Zealand	Spinning wheels
Jalfon Chemical Ltd P.O. Box 9083 Newmarket Auckland, New Zealand	Chemical dyes
New Zealand Wool Board P.O. Box 3248 Wellington, New Zealand	Fleeces
The Wheel and the Loom 144 Manukau Road Epsom, New Zealand	Spinning equipment Natural and chemical dyes Fleeces and books

Bibliography

Adrosko, Rita J. *Natural Dyes and Home Dyeing* Dover
  Publications 1968
Ary, S. and M. Gregory *The Oxford Book of Wild
  Flowers* Oxford University Press 1970
Atkinson, Frank *Some Aspects of the 18th Century Woollen
  and Worsted Trade in Halifax* Halifax Museum 1960
Bolton, Eileen M. *Lichens for Vegetable Dyeing* Studio
  Books 1960; Studio Vista 1972 and Robin and Russ
  Handweavers 1972
British Wool Marketing Board *British Sheep Breeds,
  Their Wool and Its Uses*
Brooklyn Botanic Gardens *Dye Plants and Dyeing – a
  Handbook* 1964
Brooklyn Botanic Gardens *Natural Plant Dyeing – a
  Handbook* 1973
Burnham, H. B. and D. K. *Keep Me Warm One Night*
  University of Toronto Press 1972
Cameron E. H. 'The Genius of Samuel Slater' in *The
  Technological Review* vol. 57, May 1955
Channing, Marion L. *Magic of Spinning* Marion L.
  Channing Publisher 1969
Channing Marion L. *The Textile Tools of Colonial
  Homes* Marion L. Channing Publisher 1969
CIBA Review (1939–68) CIBA Ltd, Basle
Cook, J. G. *Handbook of Textile Fibres* vol. I 'Natural
  Fibres'; vol. II 'Man-made Fibres' Textile Book
  Service 1968
Crowfoot, G. M. *Methods of Handspinning in Egypt and
  the Sudan* Bankfield Museum 1931
Davenport, Elsie G. *Your Handspinning* Craft and
  Hobby Book Service 1964
Davenport, Elsie G. *Your Yarn Dyeing* Craft and Hobby
  Book Service 1970
De Candolle, Alphonse *Origin of Cultivated Plants*
  Kegan Paul, Trench 1884; Hafner Publishing 1964
Duncan, Molly *Spin Your Own Wool* G. Bell and Sons
  1973
Duncan, Molly *Creative Crafts with Wool and Flax* G.
  Bell and Sons 1973
Earle, Alice Morse *Home Life in Colonial Days* Mac-
  millan Inc., New York 1922

English, W. *The Textile Industry* Longmans 1969 and
 Humanities Press 1970
Fannin, Allen *Handspinning: Art and Technique* Van
 Nostrand Reinhold 1971
Fennelly, Catherine *Textiles in New England 1790–1840*
 Old Sturbridge Village 1961
Fletcher, R. *Practical Mule Spinning* Emmott and Co.
 1924
Forbes, R. J. *Studies in Ancient Technology* William S.
 Heinman 1964
Grasett, K. *Guide to Handspinning* London School of
 Weaving
Haigh, H. and B. A. Newton *Wools of Britain* Pitman
 and Sons 1952
Handbook of the 'Lewis' Textile Museum Blackburn,
 England
Hay, R. and P. M. Synge *Dictionary of Garden Plants
 in Colour* Michael Joseph 1969 and Crown Publishers
 1969
Kierstead, Sallie P. *Natural Dyes* Wildwood Company
 1950
Kluger, M. *The Joy of Spinning* Simon and Schuster
 1971
Knecht, E. *A Manual of Dyeing* vol. I., Charles
 Griffen 1910
Kramer, Jack *Natural Dyes, Plants and Processes* Charles
 Scribner's Sons 1972
Lemon, H. *Lecture on Handspinning* International Wool
 Secretariat 1954
Linton, George *Modern Textile Dictionary* Textile Book
 Service 1963
Mairet, Ethel *Vegetable Dyes* Faber and Faber 1939
Martin, W. Keble *The Concise British Flora in Colour*
 Michael Joseph 1972
Merrimack Valley Textile Museum *Wool Technology
 and the Industrial Revolution* Textile Book Services 1965
Palmer, E. Laurence *Field Book of Natural History*
 McGraw-Hill Book Co. 1949
Partridge, Virginia P. *The Story of Flax* and *Dyes and
 Dyeing* N.Y.S. Historical Association, Cooperstown
Partridge, William *A Practical Treatise on Dyeing*
 Pasold Research Fund 1973
Patterson, R. *The Story of Wool, From Fleece to Yarn,
 From Yarn to Cloth*
Radcliffe, J. W. *The Manufacture of Woollen and Worsted
 Yarn* Emmott and Co. 1913
Rhind, William *A History of the Vegetable Kingdom*
 Blackie and Son 1868
Robinson, Stuart *A History of Dyed Textiles* Studio
 Vista 1969 and MIT Press 1970
Roth, H. Ling *Hand Card Making* Bankfield Museum
Roth, H. Ling *Hand Combing* Bankfield Museum .

Scott Taggard, William *Cotton Spinning* Macmillan 1919

Simmons, Paula 'Irregularity in Handspun, Part 1' in
Handweaver and Craftsman 1969

Spencer, Audrey *Spinning and Weaving at Upper Canada
Village* Ryerson Press 1964

Thompson, G. B. *Spinning Wheels (John Horner Collection)* Ulster Museum 1964

Thurstan, Violetta *The Use of Vegetable Dyes* Dryad
Press 1967

Tilton, J. K. *The History of Silk* The Scalamandre
Museum of Textiles, New York City

Ure, Andrew *A Dictionary of Arts, Manufacturers and
Mines* Longman, Orme, Brown, Green and Longmans
1839

Weir, Shelagh *Spinning and Weaving in Palestine*
British Museum 1970

Wills, Norman *Woad in the Fens* Holland Teachers'
Centre

Worst, Edward *How to Weave Linens* Bruce Co.,
Milwaukee 1931

Publications

Crafts
Crafts Advisory Committee
28 Haymarket
London SW1Y 45U, UK

Craft Horizons
American Craftmen's Council
44 West 53rd Street
New York, USA

Craftwork
Small Industries Council for Rural Areas
of Scotland
27 Walker Street
Edinburgh EH3, UK

Shuttle, Spindle and Dyepot
998 Farmingham Avenue,
West Hartford
Conn. 06107, USA

*Quarterly Journal of the Association of Guilds
of Weavers, Spinners and Dyers*
Win Evans
China Court, Church Lane
Petham, near Canterbury
Kent CT4 5RD, UK

The Web
Quarterly journal of the N.Z. Spinning,
Weaving and Woolcrafts Society
P.O. Box 192
Cambridge, New Zealand

Index

Figures in italics refer to illustrations

acetic acid 80
acrylic fibres 74, 75
Acton, Rita, *101*
adjective dyes 78
alkaline dye 80
Alkanet (*Alkanna* or *Anchusa tinctoria*) 76, *84*
alpaca *4.7*, 70, 75, *4.35*, *102*
alum 79, 81
ammonia 79
ammonium hydroxide 79
angora
  goat *4.7*, 70–1
  rabbit *4.7*, 72, *4.39*
animal fibres 54, *4.7*, 69–73
  identification of 74–5
Arkwright, Richard 17
arranging the fibres 28–35
Ashford wheel *3.19*

basin waste 73
bast fibres *see under specific plant*
Bedstraw 77, *84*
belt 43, 47
  double belted *3.17*, *3.18*, 47–8, *3.20*
  joining 43, 48
  single belted 43, *3.13*, *3.19*, 48–9,
    95, *6.9*
  size 48
  traction 43, 48, 49, 50
blaze 72
blending *2.11*, 92–3
  colour 83, 89, *6.3*, *6.4*, 92, 93
  fibres 29, *2.11*, 70, 71, 72, *6.3*, 92–3
  matchings 92
  principles 92
  texture 93, *6.3*, *6.4*
blood grades 20
Bloodroot *84*
bobbin drag *3.19*, 48–9
bobbin filling 50, 95
Boehmeria tenacissema (*B. nivea*) 67
boll (*cotton*) *4.32*, 67–8
Bombyx mori 72–3, *4.40*
boon (*flax*) 14, *4.14*
breeds *see* sheep
britch 24, *2.7*
broken mouthed 36
burning tests (*identification of fibres*)
  74–5

cabling 94–5, *6.6*
camel *4.7*, 69–70, *4.34*, 75
Cannabis sativa 66–7, *4.30*
carded wool 91
carders

clothing 28
  origin 12, 14, *1.6*
  use 28–32, *2.8–2.11*
carding
  definition 28
  origin 12, 14, *1.6*
  stages 29–32, *2.8–2.23*
  teasing 29, *2.8–2.11*
cashmere 71, *4.36*, 75
cast 36
cat hair 101
charkha 10, 68
China grass 67
Chlorophora tinctoria 85
chrome 79
classification
  blood grades 20
  fibres 54, *4.7*
  quality number 20
  sheep breeds 20
  world wool 20
clothier 16–17
combed top *2.27*, 71, 91, *6.2*
combing (*wool*) 14, 32–3, *2.24–2.27*,
  91
commercially prepared fibres 91, *6.2*
cop 43, 45, *3.16*, 96
copperas 79
Corchorus capsularis (*C. olitorius*) 66,
  4.29
Coreopsis 78, 85
correction box 50–1
cottage wheel *see* treadle
cotton *4.7*, 67–8, *4.32*, 75
  mordanting 81–2
courtelle 75
cowhair 75
cream of tartar 79, 80
crimp 20, *2.2*, 29, 92
Crompton, Samuel 17
cut 98

daggings 36
da Vinci, Leonardo 12
decortication 67
degumming silk 73
denier 98
diamond 24, *2.7*
Dipsacus fullonum 12, *1.6*
Dipsacus sylvestris 88
distaff 15, 61–4, *4.21–4.27*
diz 33, *2.27*
dog hair *4.7*, 72, *101*
donning on 32, *2.24*
drafting (*drawing out*) zone *3.1*, 38,

40, *3.10–3.11*, 41, 44, 45, *3.15*, 49,
  50, *3.22–3.23*, 50–1, *4.3–4.6*, 68,
  6.1, 94, 95
drying, wool 27
  yarn 98
dyeing 76–89
  collecting dyestuffs 77
  dyestuffs, guide 84–8
  equipment 77–8
  fastness 89
  methods 82–3
  mordanting 78–82
  preparation 77–8
  records 89
  variations 89
dyestuffs, guide 84–8

ewe 36
experimenting
  fibres 54–75
  techniques 52–4
extra diamond *2.7*, 26

fallen/fell wool 36
fancy yarns *6.3*, *6.4*, *6.6*
fastness of dyes 89
felting 27
ferrous sulphate 79
fibres
  animal 54, *4.7*
  arrangement 28–35, *2.8–2.32*
  bast *4.7*, 55–67
  classification *4.7*, 54
  commercially prepared 91, *6.2*
  fruit *4.7*, 67–8
  identification 74–5
  leaf *4.7*, 68
  man-made *4.7*, 54, 74
  natural *4.7*, 55–73
  seed *4.7*, 67–8
  vegetable *4.7*, 55–68
fibre supply 38, *3.1*, 40, *3.9*, 42–3,
  44–5, *3.14*, 49–51, *3.21–3.22*, *4.1*,
  90, *6.1*, 94
filament 74
Filipendula ulmaria 80, *87*
fineness (*degree of*) 20, 36
flax 6, *4.7–4.8*, 55–66, *4.14*, 75
  bleaching 64, 66
  breaking 14, 61, *4.16–4.17*
  colour 61
  cross section *4.14*
  description 55, *4.8*
  dressing the distaff 61–4, *4.21–4.27*
  grassing 59, *4.15*, 64–5

hackling 6, *4.19*, 61, *4.20*
jelly 64, *4.28*
line 61, 64, *4.20*, *4.22*, *101*
mordanting 81–2
preparation (*history*) 14–15
processing 55–61, *4.11–4.20*
queue 61 *see* strick
scouring 64, 66, 96, 98
scutching 14, 18, *4.18*, 61
spinning 64, *4.28*
strick 61–3, *4.21*
tools 14–15, *4.13*, *4.16–4.20*
tow 61, *4.20*, 64
fleece
   guide 22–3
   parts 24–6, *2.7*
   scouring 26–7
   selection 21–3
   sorting 21, 24–6, *2.3–2.7*
   suitability 22–3
   terms 19, 36–7
   weight 22–3
flyer assembly *1.5*, 12, 45, 47, *3.7*, *3.9*, *3.20*, 48
flyer wheel *see* treadle
Fustic *85*

Galium verum 77, *84*
garnett yarn *6.3*, 93
ginned cotton 68
goat *4.7*, 70–1, *4.36*, 75
Golden rod 79, *86*
Gossypium species 67–8, *4.32*
grassing 59, *4.15*, 64–5
great wheel
   maintenance 43
   origin 10, 12
   parts 44, *3.13*
   use 44–5, *3.14–3.16*, 68, 95, *6.9*
green vitriol 79

hackle, heckle (*flax*) 14–15, 59, *4.19–4.20*, 61
   (*wool*) 34, *2.28–2.29*
Haematoxylon campechianum 86
hair *4.7*, 69–73, 75
half hitch 39, 40, *3.7–3.8*
handle of wool 36
handspun 94, 96, 99, *100–103*
hank 98
Hargreaves, James 17
Hayes, Sylvia *101*, *102*, *103*
hemp *4.7*, 66–7, *4.30*, 75
high wheel *see* great
history of spinning 9–18
hogg, hoggets 36
horsehair 75
Hypericum species 82, 87

identification of fibres 74–5
India, charkha 10
iron 79
Isatis tinctoria 89

jack (*spinning*) 17
jenny
   combing 14
   spinning 17
jigging 32, *2.25*
Jugen, Johann 12
jute *4.7*, 66, *4.29*, 75

kapok 75
karakul 75
Kashmir goat *see* cashmere
kemp 21, 36
knitting 99, *101*
knubbs 72–3

lace *101*
lanolin, replacing 27–8
lea 98
leaf fibres *4.7*, 68
line, linen *see flax*
Linum usitatissimum 55–66, *4.8*
llama *4.7*, 70
lock (*wool*) 19, *2.2*, *2.10*
Logwood *86*
long draw 52–4, *4.1–4.6*
long wheel 10 *see also* great
low wheel *see* treadle
lustre (*degree of*) 36

Madder *86*
manila 75
man-made fibres 54, *4.7*, 74
Marigold *86*
marijuana 67
Meadowsweet *87*
metallic salts 79–81
Minor's head 12, *1.4*, *3.13–3.16*
mohair *see* angora goat
moths 26, 70
mordanting 78–82
   cotton 81–2
   linen 81–2
   methods 81
   silk 82
muckle wheel 10 *see* great
mule (*cotton*) 17
multiplying head *1.4*, 12, *3.13–3.16*
musk-ox *4.7*, 71–2, *4.38*

natural dyes *see* dyeing
natural polymers 54, *4.7*, 74
nettles *4.7*, 67, *4.31*
New Zealand flax 5, 68, *4.33*
niddy noddy *1.7*, 16, 96, *6.11*
noilage 32, *2.26*
noils 32, *2.29*, *6.3*, 93
novelty yarns *6.3*, *6.4*, *6.6*
nylon 75

oiling 27, 28, 52, 68
olive oil emulsion 28
orifice 49, 50, 95, *6.8*
orlon 75
overtwist 51, *6.4*, 93

Phormium tenax 68, *4.33*
plying 94–5, *6.6–6.9*
polyacrilonitrile fibres 75
potassium aluminium sulphate 79
potassium bichromate or dichromate 79
prime 24, *2.7*

quality number 20, 22–3, 70
queue *see* flax
qiviut *see* musk-ox

rabbit (*angora*) *4.7*, 72, *4.39*
Ragwort *81*, *87*
ram 37

ramie *4.7*, 67, 75
rayon 75
reconditioning wool 27–8
Reed, Tony *100*
reel
   click *1.7*
   stick *1.7*, *6.11*
   use 16, *6.11*, 96
Reseda luteola 83, *89*
retting 59, 61, *4.15*
Rhus species 88
rippling *4.13*
rooed 36, 72
roving 35, *2.32*, 91
Rubia tinctorium 86
ruffler *4.19*, 61

Saint John's wort *82*, *87*
Sanguinaria canadensis 84
saxony wheel *see* treadle
scale (*wool*) *2.1–2.2*, 19–20
scotch tension *3.19*, 48–9
scouring 96, 98
   cotton 73, 98
   linen 64, 66, 96, 98
   silk 73, 96
   wool 26–7, 94, 96, 98
scutching 14, *4.18*, 16
second cuts 21, 29, *2.9*, 35, 93
seed and fruit fibres *4.7*, 67–8
semi-worsted *2.8–2.9*, 34–5, *2.30–2.32*, 90–1, 92
Senecio jacobaea 81, *87*
sericin 79
shearing 12
sheep
   breeds 22–3
   classification 20
   terms 36–7
short draw *3.20–3.23*, 49–50, 52, 54, 69–70, 71, 91, *6.2*, 95
silk *4.7*, *4.40*
   cultivation 72–3
   degumming 73
   mordanting 82
   scouring 73
   tussah or wild 73, 75
   waste 72–3, 75
sisal 68, 75
skeining *1.7*, 45, 96, *6.10–6.13*
sliver 73, 91
slubs *6.4*, 93
sodium carbonate 81
Solidago species 79, *86*
sorting a fleece 21–6, *2.3–2.7*, 36–7
spindle (*hand*)
   half-hitch 39, 40, *3.7–3.8*
   origin 9–10
   plying 94–5
   types 39, *3.2*
   use 39–43, *3.3–3.12*, 94–5
   whorls 9–10, *1.1–1.2*, 39
spindle (*mechanized*) 10–11
   accelerated *1.4*
   direct drive *1.3*
   horizontally mounted 10, 12, 43
spinning
   commercially prepared fibres 91, *6.2*
   long draw 52–4, *4.1–4.6*
   on great wheel 44–5, *3.14–3.16*, 95, *6.9*

on spindle 39–43, *3.3–3.12*, 94–5
on treadle wheel 45–50, *3.20–3.23*, 52–4, *4.1–4.6*, *6.7–6.8*, 95
principles 38, *3.1*, 43
problems 50–1
semi-worsted *2.8–2.9*, 34–5, *2.30–2.32*, 90–1, 92
short draw 49–50, *3.20–3.23*, 69–70, 71, 91, 93, 95
short stapled fibres 68, 71
woollen 39–50, *3.3–3.12*, *3.14–3.16*, *3.20–3.23*, 52–4, *4.1–4.6*
worsted 34, 48, 90–1, *6.2*
spinning wheels *see* wheels
springiness (*degree of*) 36
stannous chloride 79–80
staple 20, *2.2*
staple length 20, 22–3, 37
strength 37
strick *see* flax
suint 37
scutching 14, 18, *4.18*, 61
S twist 64, 94, *6.5–6.6*, 95, *6.9*
substantive dyes 78
Sumac *88*
swingling 14, 18, *4.18*, 61
synthetics 54, *4.7*, 74, 75

Tagetes species 86
Tanacetum vulgare 88
tannic acid 80, 81
Tansey *88*
teasels 12, *1.6*, *88*
teasing
    before carding *2.8–2.10*, 29
    instead of carding 35, *2.30–2.32*
tegs 37
tension, adjustment 47–9, 50–1
tex system 99
textile industry
    America 17–18, 91
    Britain 16–17, 91
texture 51, 91–4, *6.3–6.5*
tie dyeing 89
tin 79–80
top (*combed*) 33, *2.27*, 34, *6.2*, 91
top dyeing 89
tow
    flax 61, *4.20*
    man-made 94
treadle wheel

double belted *3.17–3.18*, 47–8
origin 12
parts *3.17–3.19*
single belted 48–9, *3.19*
upright *3.18*
use 45–50, 52–4, *3.20–3.23*, *4.1–4.6*, *6.7–6.8*, 95
treadling problems 50–1
tup 37
tussah silk 73, 75
twist
    amount 38, *3.1*, 47, 48, 49, 50–1, 69, 94
    degree 93, *6.4*
    S twist *6.5*, 94, 95, *6.9*
    Z twist 40, 45, *6.5–6.6*, 94, 95, *6.9*
twisting zone 38, *3.1*, *3.11*, *3.15*, *3.22*
two shear/toothed 37

U-flyer 12, *1.5*, 45, 47, *3.17–3.20*, 48–9
upright wheel *see* treadle
Urticaceae species 67, *4.31*

vegetable dyes *see* dyeing
vegetable fibres 54, *4.7*, 55–68
vicuna 70
vinegar 80

warp yarn 94, *101*, *102*
water frame 17
weaving with handspun 94, 99, *100–2*
weft yarn 94, *100–2*
Weld *83*, *89*
wether/wedder 37
wheels
    Ashford *3.19*
    bobbin and flyer 12, *1.5*, 45, 47, *3.17–3.20*, 48–9
    bobbin drag *3.19*, 48–9
    charkha 10, 68
    great wheel 10, 12, 43–5, *3.14–3.16*, 68, 95, *6.9*
    long wheel 10
    muckle wheel 10
    origin 10, 12
    scotch tension *3.19*, 48–9
    treadle 45–50, *3.17–3.23*, 52–4, *4.1–4.6*, *6.7–6.8*, 95
    upright *3.18*
    walking 10, 12, *3.13*

wool 10, *3.13*
whorls 9–10, *1.1–1.2*, *3.2*
Woad *89*
wool
    calculations 28–9
    characteristics 19–20, *2.1*, 75
    classification 20, *4.7*
    crimp 20, *2.2*, 29, 91
    drying 27, 98
    fleece 19, 21–6, *2.3–2.7*, 36–7
    inferior 91
    microscopic construction 19, *2.1*
    quality number 20
    scouring 26–7, 94, 96, 98
    storage 26
    tender 21
    term 69
woollen
    characteristics 32, *6.1*
    commercially prepared 91, *6.2*
    preparation 28–32
    spinning 39–50, *3.3–3.12*, *3.14–3.16*, *3.20–3.23*, 52–4, *4.1–4.6*
Wool Marketing Board 21
wool wheel 10
World Classification of Wool 20
worsted
    characteristics 32–4, *6.1*, 90–1
    commercially prepared 91, *6.2*
    preparation 32–4, *2.24–2.29*
    spinning 34, 48, 90–1, *6.2*

yak *4.7*, 71, *4.37*
yarn
    breakage 51
    cabling 94–5, *6.6*
    count 38, 45, 98–9
    design 52, 90–103, *6.3*, *6.4*, *6.6*
    determining twist 38, 51, 93, 94
    plying 94–5, *6.6–6 9*
    scouring 96, 98
    semi-worsted 34–5, 90–1, *6.1*
    thickness 38, 45, 51
    woollen 32, 90–1, *6.1*, 94
    worsted 32–33, 90–1, *6.1*, 94
    use 94, 96, 99, *100–3*
yarn package 43, 45, *3.16*, 96
yarn winders *see* reels
    yield 37

Z twist 40, 45, *6.5–6.6*, 94, 95, *6.9*